535

ANTIQUE WEAPONS

---

for pleasure and investment

ANTIQUE
WEAPONS

for pleasure
and investment

By RICHARD AKEHURST

JOHN GIFFORD LTD · LONDON

First published in Great Britain by
John Gifford Ltd., 125 Charing Cross Road,
London W.C.2.

SBN 70710241 3

Text and plates printed in Great Britain
by Compton Printing Ltd.
London and Aylesbury

Acknowledgements

The author and publishers wish to thank the following for their kind help with the illustrations:

Frank Anderson Esq., Colour Plates: 5, 19. Plates: 27, 89 photographed by C. Crosthwaite Esq.

Author, Colour Plates: 6, 10, 11, 13, 14, 18, 20, 22, 23, 24. Plates: 29, 43, 53, 55, 56, 58, 63, 80, 93, 95, 96, 97 photographed by C. Crosthwaite Esq.

Christie's, Plates: 92, 98, 99, 100

Peter Dale Ltd., Plates: 1, 2, 3, 5, 6, 7, 8, 11, 12, 13, 17, 19, 20, 21, 22, 26, 39, 42, 44, 45, 46, 59, 61, 66, 67, 69, 71, 75, 76, 84, 85, 86, 94, 104

Frost & Reed Ltd., Colour Plate: 12

John McMaster, Colour Plates: 8, 9

W. Keith Neal Esq., Colour Plates: 1, 2, 3, 4, 7, 15, 16, 17, 21. Plates: 14, 18, 30, 32, 33, 34, 35, 36, 37, 40, 49, 51, 52, 54, 57, 60, 62, 79, 82, 83, 90 photographed by owner.

Sotheby's, Plates: 4, 9, 10, 15, 16, 25, 28, 47, 48, 50, 68, 101, 103

Wallis & Wallis, Plates: 31, 65, 72, 73, 77, 78, 81, 87, 88, 91, 102, 104

CONTENTS

Introduction   1

1. European personal weapons   5

2. Military and naval weapons   47

3. Sporting weapons   77

4. Weapons of the American frontier   103

5. Weapons of the Near East   119

6. Weapons of India and Indonesia   135

7. Weapons of Japan   149

8. Some hints on the restoration of weapons   163

List of Colour Plates

1   Pair of flintlock travelling pistols by William Smith, London *circa* 1800, in original case with fittings including powder flask and bullet mould.

2   Flintlock over and under double-barrelled pocket pistol by Joseph Egg, London *circa* 1820, in original velvet-lined case with fittings including powder flask, patch box, bullet mould, loading rod and spare flints.

3   Pair of under-hammer percussion pocket pistols by Pirmet, Paris *circa* 1830, constructed to give a clear line of sight. In original case with all fittings, including key for unscrewing the turn-off barrels, powder flask, bullet mould and nipple key.

4   Silver-mounted pepperbox by Samuel and Charles Smith, London, in original velvet-lined case with all fittings including nipple key, powder flask, bullet mould and spare nipples. The Birmingham silver mark is for 1846, London proof marks.

5   Brass-barrelled flintlock blunderbuss with top spring bayonet, by P. Whitney, Cork *circa* 1800 and embossed gun-metal sporting powder flask.

6   Pair of two-groove rifled percussion target pistols by James Purdey, London, engraved 'Made for the Maharajah of Bulrampore 1864.' Leaf sights for 20, 40, 60, 80 and 100 yards. These fine pistols were recently brought back from India uncased; the case was fitted in velvet and gold tooled leather and fittings made in silver, ivory, etc., by the author.

7   Scottish weapons: Highland snaphaunce all metal pistol with heart-shaped butt by I. O. Stuart *circa* 1690, Broadsword with basket hilt *circa* 1660 and Targe *circa* 1745.

8   Charge of the 2nd, the Royal North British Dragoons at Waterloo 1815. Known as the Scots Greys they became officially The Royal Scots Greys in 1877. Colour lithograph.

9   The 57th, the Duke of Cambridge's Own (Middlesex) shown with their spiked helmets and Martini-Henry rifles and bayonets. Colour lithograph from 'Her Majesty's Army, 1889.'

10   *Right:* Dirk carried by Midshipman Patton at the Battle of Trafalgar, 1805, hilt ivory with gilt bronze quillons and mounts. For comparison left: 20th-century Midshipman's dirk, now obsolete; last worn at the Coronation 1953.

11   16-bore flintlock sporting gun by John Manton, London. Made in 1820 for the 6th Duke of Bedford. Fine example of late flintlock with rainproof 'V' pan, spur cock and cutaway breech. French horn powder flask 19th century.

12   Sportsman loading percussion gun, his shot belt over his shoulder and his tin-plate powder flask beside his game-bag. Oil painting by Richard Ansdell *circa* 1830.

13   16-bore, two-groove sporting rifle by Joseph Lang, London, 1853. 32-in. stub-twist barrel; originally all other ironwork gilt, now mostly worn off showing burnished iron. Made for a Maharajah. Complete in case with fittings. Bullet mould, tang clipper, belted balls, patches and powder measure are shown.

List of Colour Plates

14 'The Old Shekarry' (H. A. Leveson) well armed with two percussion double rifles having a desperate battle with a black bear in India in the 1840s. Colour lithograph from 'Wild Sports'.

15 Flintlock Kentucky rifle by S. Miller of Pennsylvania *circa* 1815. Typical ripple grained stock and large decorative patch box. Engraved cow-horn flask *c*. 1775 shows New York and on reverse side the *Royal George*, ship of the line.

16 Navy pattern colt, extra engraved, presented by Samuel Colt in 1851. A large number of this pattern were ordered by the British Government for the Navy. Shown in original velvet-lined case with all fittings.

17 Superb pair of Cossack pistols *circa* 1840 with leather-covered stock, gold inlaid locks and barrels, silver gilt mounts inlaid with neillo and ivory ball butts. The lock is the Cossack version of the Spanish or Miquelet lock. Also shown is a priming flask.

18 Arabian jambiya, heavily silver mounted, the hilt of rhinoceros horn embedded with silver nails. The lower scabbard covered with interlaced flat silver wire. Formally worn by an Arab Dhow captain.

19 *Left:* Large Indo-Persian dagger having some affinity to the Kyber knife with ivory hilt and fine Persian 'watered' steel blade, scabbard covered with velvet with bronze gilt mounts. *Right:* Silver mounted Kukri from Nepal decorated with the arms of the Gurkha Rifles. Hilt of buffalo horn.

20 Akbar Shar (1556-1605), greatest of the Mughal Emperors of India, shown wearing his favourite dagger, the katar, in his sash. Mughal miniature painting.

21 Indian weapons: a typical good-quality matchlock gun (toradar) with iron powder flask; also two fine examples of the broad-bladed thrusting dagger (katar), one with enamelled decoration, the other damascened with gold.

22 Japanese battle scene by moonlight between Samurai in civil costume, showing style of swordplay in which great agility and some use of the blade to parry were the means of avoiding a cut or thrust. Woodcut print.

23 Japanese wakizashi blade (unsigned) with deep groove and billowing hardened edge (yakiba) of the type known as 'sugu-chojiha,' typical of many of the later blades made by the renowned smiths of Osafune in Bizen province in the 17th century. Also shown are two sword guards (tsuba) and an arrowhead with a pierced design of plum blossom.

24 The last stand of the one-eyed general Yamamoto Kansuke in the campaign of Kawana-kajima in 1561. Note the general's slung long sword (tachi) and dagger (tanto) and his black war fan, the equivalent of a marshal's baton. Also note the straight-bladed spears (su yari). Woodcut print.

List of Black & White Photographs

1.	English rapier, *circa* 1620	6
2.	Spanish cup-hilted rapier, early 17th century	9
3.	Italian left-hand dagger with sheath, late 16th century	10
4.	Left: French smallsword, late 17th century. Centre: French smallsword, third quarter of 17th century. Right: French smallsword, late 18th century	12
5.	English silver hilted smallsword, 1750	14
6.	English silver hilted smallsword, 1750	17
7.	English broadsword, mid-17th century	18
8.	English flintlock holster pistol by Thomas Green, *circa* 1690	20
9.	French flintlock holster pistols by Frenel of Paris, early 18th century	21
10.	English turn-off pocket pistols by E. Gifford, late 17th century	22
11.	English flintlock turn-off, cannon barrelled pistols, *circa* 1750	23
12.	English flintlock turn-off, cannon barrelled pistol by J. Freeman, *circa* 1750	25
13.	English turn-off flintlock pocket pistol, *circa* 1800	26
14.	Silver mounted duelling pistols by Robert Wogdon, 1774	28
15.	Silver mounted flintlock presentation duelling pistols by John Manton, *circa* 1810	29
16.	Flintlock presentation pistols by Bennett and Lacy, 1811	31
17.	Over and under officers' pistols by John Manton and Sons, *circa* 1812	33
18.	Double barrelled over and under pistol by Staudenmayer, London, *circa* 1810	34
19.	Pepperbox pistol by W. & J. Rigby	35
20.	J. R. Cooper's patent pepperbox, *circa* 1845	36
21.	Transitional revolver, *circa* 1850	37
22.	Baker's Patent transitional revolver, *circa* 1852	38
23.	William Tranter's percussion revolver	39
24.	Philip Webley's percussion revolver	40
25.	Pellet lock target pistols by Le Page of Paris, mid- 1820s	41
26.	Percussion target or duelling pistols by Le Page of Paris, mid-19th century	42
27.	Skean dhu. silver mounted	44

28. Pair of Scottish all steel flintlock pistols by John Campbell, *circa* 1750   45

29. Major General Warde and Infantry of the Waterloo period   49

30. Lock of Brown Bess musket, *circa* 1810   50

31. Upper: India pattern Brown Bess musket. Lower: ·773 Military percussion carbine, 1838   51

32. Dragoon pistol, 1743   52

33. Cavalry pistol, *circa* 1815   54

34. Military Highland pistol by Christie of Doune, *circa* 1765   55

35. The Duke of Richmond's pattern musket, *circa* 1790   56

36. Military Ferguson breech-loading rifle by Durs Egg, *circa* 1780   57

37. The Baker rifle   58

38. Rifleman of the 95th or Rifle Regiment   60

39. 1856 Pattern rifled military pistol, dated 1859   62

40. Adams' percussion revolver ·50 calibre, *circa* 1851   63

41. Adams' central fire breech-loading regulation army pattern revolver of 1867   63

42. Heavy cavalry officer's dress sword pattern of 1796   65

43. Stirrup hilted sabre, early 19th century   66

44. Stirrup hilted sabre, Peninsular War   68

45. Officer's Spadroon of the Loyal St James's Volunteers (raised 1797)   71

46. Left: Naval Officer's regulation pattern sword of 1805–1827. Centre: Naval Officer's regulation pattern sword of 1805–1827. Right: Naval Officer's sword 1827 pattern   73

47. Lloyd's Patriotic Fund Sword of the fifty pound type   74

48. Fine English presentation sabre, 1797   76

49. English hunting sword combined with a pistol, *circa* 1740   78

50. Spanish flintlock gun, 1758   81

51. Detail of silver wire inlay on an English fowling piece by Delany, 1725   82

52. Light 28 bore fowling piece by Sikes of Sheffield, *circa* 1775   85

53. Engraving from The Shooting Directory by Thornhill, 1804, showing sportsman priming the pan   86

54. Double barrelled flintlock gun by John Manton, *circa* 1800   88

55. Engraving of pheasant shooting, from The Shooting Directory by Thornhill, 1804   89

56. Double barrelled percussion sporting gun by James Purdey 1837   90

57. Double barrelled 12 bore pinfire gun by John Dickson of Edinburgh, 1863   92

58. Double barrelled 12 bore centre fire gun by Pape of Newcastle, *circa* 1868   93

59. Silesian Tschinke, 17th century   94

60. German flintlock Jäger rifle, *circa* 1700   95

61. English single barrel percussion sporting rifle, *circa* 1830 by Nock   96

62. English percussion double barrelled rifle by James Purdey, 1844   97

63. Two-groove sporting rifle by Joseph Lang, London, 1853   99

64. A tricky situation when elephant hunting in the days of the muzzle-loader   100

65. Double-barrelled ·500 breech-loading hammer rifle by W. T. Jeffrey & Co., *circa* 1880s   102

66. Kentucky flintlock rifle by Jacob Kunts of Philadelphia, Pennsylvania (1770–1817)   104

67. Colt 'Texas' Paterson holster pistol of ·36 calibre, *circa* 1840   105

68. Colt Walker-Whitney Dragoon revolver of ·44 calibre, dated 1847   106

69. Engraved Colt Model 1849 Pocket Pistol   109

70. Riding down a buffalo using a heavy calibre revolver   110

71. English Bowie knife made for the American market by Edward Barnes and Sons, Sheffield, mid-19th century   112

72. Upper: Winchester model, 1866. Middle: Winchester model, 1866, engraved. Lower: Spencer ·56 rimfire repeating rifle. First patented 1860   113

73. American embossed 'Peace' powder flask   114

74. Annie Oakley with her Winchester repeating rifle   115

75. Henry Deringer's original pistol, first introduced in the 1830s   116

76. Remington double deringer with over and under rifled ·41 calibre barrels   117

77. Upper: Cossack dagger. Middle: Turkish sword. Lower: Turkish sabre or Kilij   120

78. Upper: Arab sword. Middle: Turkish Yataghan. Lower: Turkish Kilij   122

79. Persian dagger, *circa* 1800   124
80. North African style miquelet lock   125
81. Upper: Typical Turkish style gun. Lower: Balkan gun   127
82. Turkish Damascus twist barrel   128
83. Signed Turkish Damascus twist barrel   129
84. Turkish or Balkan pistol   130
85. North African (Moroccan?) flintlock pistol, *circa* 1800   131
86. Typical short Turkish blunderbuss, early 19th century   132
87. Two decorative Indian Katars   134
88. Upper: Khanda. Middle: Combined spike axe and dagger of crutch type. Lower: Small crutch sword   136
89. Detail of Indo-Persian knife blade showing watered steel   137
90. Indian dagger with strengthened back rib and diamond sectioned armour piercing point   138
91. Left to right: Indian jambiya, Indian jambiya with watered steel panels, Indian all steel dagger, Indian dagger with gilt blade and hilt   139
92. Left: A fine mutton fat jade Khanjar hilt. Centre: A fine Indian Khanjar. Right: Fine Javanese gold kris hilt   141
93. Sabre with fine watered steel blade and tiger headed hilt   142
94. Beaumont-Adams percussion revolver, *circa* 1858, damascened in gold   143
95. Fine example of a laminated Javanese blade   144
96. Javanese kris with stylised Garuda hilt carved in wood   146
97. Javanese sword   147
98. Wakizashi blade by Sukenao of Osaka, 17th century   151
99. Wakizashi blade by Yoshimichi, *circa* 1600   152
100. Tsuba of the 18th and 19th centuries   155
101. Left: Kogai. Middle: Kodsuka. Right: Sword hilt Lower: Tsuba   156
102. Yoroi-toshi, a dagger with a thick armour piercing blade   157
103. Three wakizashi (upper) and three katana (lower)   159
104. Upper: Typical Japanese matchlock gun. Lower: Japanese matchlock gun with inlaid barrel   161

Introduction

There is a fascination about old weapons, their association with the romance of past times, their graceful fitness for purpose, their fine or curious ornament, the strange and sometimes bizarre shapes of weapons from distant lands.

An interest in collecting old weapons may start at an early age or may be awakened by the odd purchase of an interesting piece found in an antique shop or perhaps with family weapons handed on, or weapons brought home from abroad. However the collector starts, it is certain that interest and enthusiasm will increase as his knowledge of the weapons is enlarged.

In the first instance many collectors dabble here and there buying as and when opportunity occurs, at a price they can afford. This sort of preliminary exploration on a broad front is of great value in widening the basic knowledge and gaining experience in buying; and later selling experience as some of the odds and ends are sold in order to buy better items.

The question of value is inseparable from collecting; and this question of value may be divided into two main parts: first monetary value and second intrinsic value, both important and often closely related. Taking monetary value first, there

1

are a few basic points to be made: the price of a weapon depends on its desirability and the quantity available, rarity alone will not necessarily bring a high value. Some weapons may have a special value because they were made by a famous maker, or they were used on historic or interesting occasions, or belonged to a notable person, even the fact that they were once in an important collection may influence value. Where, for instance, a collection of a particular type of arm would be incomplete without a rare item of particular interest, such items are bound to fetch very high prices.

In considering the intrinsic value of a weapon a collector can assess its value to him as an item of interest. This is the most desirable aspect of valuation since it is through the seeking for knowledge, inspired by the first interest, that the greatest pleasure and satisfaction is to be derived.

Sheer acquisitiveness or buying only as a means of making money are sterile aspects of collecting and not to be encouraged since they lead to items being bought and locked away solely to await an increase in value. This has the effect of denying items to the genuine collector and also of pushing up prices.

It would of course be unrealistic to suppose that most collectors do not have an eye to buying well, hoping to make a profit if they should sell later. This not only adds a certain spice to the game, but also as the majority of collectors are not wealthy people, it increases the capital enabling further and finer items to be added to the collection.

All this is fine if the collector is really interested in the item at the time that he buys and intends to keep it long enough for appreciation in value to take place. Where the beginner can go astray is in dabbling in items of which he has scant knowledge merely because he thinks they may be valuable. Sometimes luck may be with him but there is much to guard against even for those with considerable knowledge, and whereas all collectors must expect to pay something for experience, no one wants to pay too much.

Now assuming that the collector, fired with enthusiasm for weapons, sets out with a certain amount of spare money to add further items, there are several possibilities open to him: he can hunt through the well known street markets, the 'junk' shops, newspaper advertisements, provincial sale rooms and even

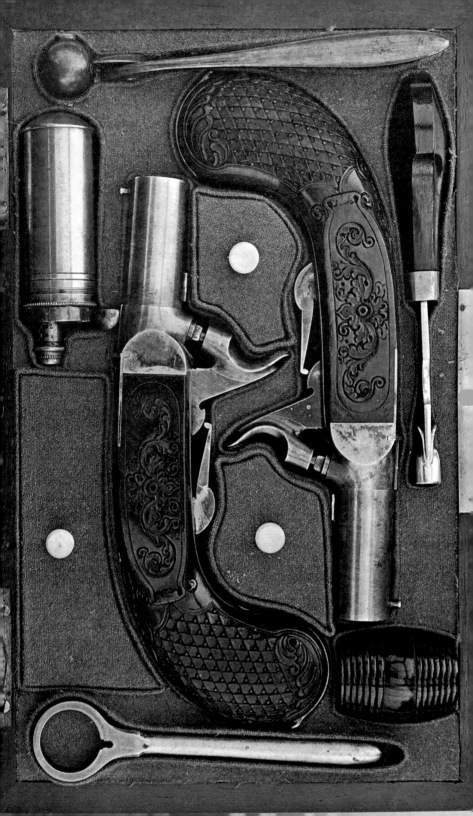

jumble sales and 'antique' stalls at fetes. This may appeal to those with time to spare and there is also the joy of the hunt and the vision of a real find to spur them on.

For those with less time and rather more money there are antique shops in general and those that have the odd weapons now and then in particular. There are also the sale rooms that specialise in antique weapons where a large selection of weapons can be viewed. The collector can try his hand at bidding for himself at the sale or can instruct a dealer or the saleroom staff to bid for him. Some salerooms take postal bids and those that issue lists giving the prices realised are particularly useful for they enable a collector to keep in touch with the current price levels of various items. It should be remembered that many of the bidders at auctions will be dealers and should items they buy subsequently be offered for sale by them, they will have to add a fair margin for profit to the price, but then a private buyer may have to pay more at a sale anyway when in competition with the trade.

The collector whose time is limited, who has moderate to large funds available and wishes to collect only items of good quality, will do best to patronise a reliable specialist dealer. He will perhaps pay more when buying from a specialist, but not always, and he has the advantage of the specialist's knowledge and he will be able to select from a wider variety. This is certainly the safest way to collect if knowledge is limited and considerable sums of money involved. Also a good dealer will keep, for his best customers, items that they particularly want.

Even when a collector has considerable knowledge, he will be wise to buy important items from a recognised dealer who is prepared to guarantee their authenticity. There are so many pitfalls for the unwary antique collector and weapons are no exception. With increasing shortages and higher prices the temptation is greater to pass off as original varying degrees of 'restoration' and even skilfully made reproductions.

Dealers regularly visit general antique shops, that is either the main dealer himself or the roaming dealers that frequently bring him anything of interest, therefore if a weapon has stayed for a long time in a general shop the likelihood is that it is either a 'wrong one' or the price is too high. Sometimes provincial antique shops, getting a weapon they have not seen before, overestimate its value or put an unduly high price on it because they do not know its current price. A similar weapon may be cheaper in a specialist's shop.

Interesting weapons often turn up in varying degrees of bad condition, and although there was a time when these would be passed over, now that perfect specimens are scarce and expensive it becomes well worth spending time restoring weapons to a state as near their former glory as is possible.

In restoring a weapon the greatest caution must be exercised, for more harm than good can so easily be done. In general, any original finish should be preserved and any slight areas of rust, for instance, removed with the greatest care. Some guidance on the restoration of various types of weapon will follow in a later chapter treating this aspect in detail. It is however wise to gain experience on items of little value and progress to the more important when skill and confidence have been gained. In the area of skilled restoration, those inclined towards craftsmanship may find both the greatest satisfaction and also the greatest appreciation of the art of the weapon maker.

Much pleasure can be gained and knowledge added by collecting books, paintings and prints relating to, and contemporary with, the weapons which most interest the collector.

Colour plate 3
Under-hammer pistol, Pirmet

1. European personal weapons

Of all the personal weapons used in Europe, the sword retained a special place, from the Viking straight two-edged sword to the small sword. The Viking sword was developed into the weapon of the armed knight and became the symbol of honour, justice and kingly power.

In early times the art of the swordsmith was woven with legend and superstition; fire, water and hammer blows combined to produce some blades that were obviously better than others, so it was not surprising that the intervention of supernatural power was assumed.

As the blades of the Ancient heroes excelled in the testing trials of battle, so were born the stories of magical swords invincible in combat that endowed with the same spirit all who wielded them; such was 'Naegling', the legendary sword of Beowulf, 'Durindal' the sword of Roland, most famed of Charlemagne's knights, and all know of King Arthur's 'Excalibur'.

The forging method used for some of these sword blades, possibly made in the region of the Rhine, is most interesting. In order to ensure strength and resilience combined with a hard cutting edge, the central part of the blade was composed of

5

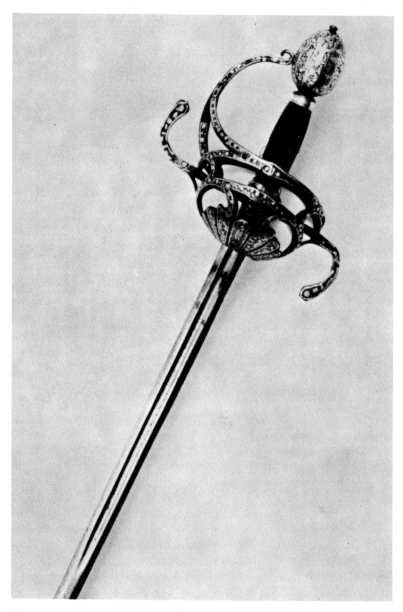

Plate 1
Fine quality English rapier *circa* 1620. The
hilt richly inlaid with silver in high relief.

strips of alternate iron and low carbon steel twisted together and laid side by side; then to the outer edges were laid the steel strips for the cutting edge and point. The whole was then forge welded and hammered to condense and harden the metal.

The straight double-edged sword of diamond section or with a central groove, large pommel and with the quillons either straight or curved towards the blade, became the standard fighting sword associated with the armed knights of the age of chivalry, of Charlemagne's knights and those of the crusades.

In the fourteenth and fifteenth centuries, especially for fighting on foot, a great two-handed sword was sometimes used or as a compromise the hand-and-half sword which could be used one or two handed as occasion served. Also in these times the battle axe, mace and flail were favourite weapons for battering plate armour. From the beginning of the fourteenth century some swords had been designed with more emphasis on thrusting in order to find weak places between the joints of plate armour. This type culminated in the development of the thrusting sword known as the rapier (plate 1). With the increased use of firearms and therefore the use of less and lighter armour the art of fencing was developed; a technique which enabled a blade to serve for defence as well as offence. The need for free movement of the wrist and fingers for this style of sword-play led to the disguarding of the armoured gauntlet. To protect the hand a variety of guards were built on the hilt and the top of the blade was left unsharpened where the forefinger rested on it, as it had to if the fingers were correctly positioned for thrusting.

The typical sixteenth-century rapier is sometimes referred to as 'swept hilted' on account of the bold S-shaped sweep of the quillons round the knuckles to the pommel, and at the other end curved forward over the blade. The hilt developed in the seventeenth century through intermediate stages to the classic form of the cup-hilted rapier with straight quillons. The cup hilt was often enriched with intricate pierced and chiselled designs (plate 2). The blade, of wonderfully tempered steel, was lighter, more narrow and designed to be used entirely with the point.

Because of the length of the rapier blade it was essential to have a left hand dagger to guard against a dagger being used by an opponent when a sword thrust was parried, the dagger could then be used to parry the opponent's dagger (plate 3).

These left hand daggers were often made en suite with the rapier, but the need for them disappeared when in the middle of the seventeenth century the smallsword (plate 4), aided by the fencing technique which made it such a deadly weapon, replaced the rapier.

The typical smallsword blade was much shorter than the rapier and by the eighteenth century of a hollow ground triangular shape, often expanding to a wider flatter shape towards the hilt. The hilt was furnished with a butterfly-shaped guard, and one of the light quillons was swept round to the pommel to act as a knuckle guard. These small swords became the accepted part of the dress of a gentleman in the late seventeenth and eighteenth centuries and were enriched with varying degrees of splendour according to the taste of the times. The enriched iron of the earlier guards gave place to the use of silver, gold or copper gilt, chased ornament and enamelling. For all those keen on fencing the original forms of the épée and foil must have a special interest, but they also have a particular attraction as works of art, graceful in overall shape and proportion and interesting for their variety of ornament. Having a hall marked silver guard enables the collector to find the exact date and maker of the silver work (plates 5 and 6).

An interesting basket-hilted broadsword was used by Venetian mercenaries in the seventeenth century called the Schiavona the 'basket' being formed from diagonally crossed iron straps and the pommel of a flattened decorative brass shape. Of great interest because of their use in the Civil War between Charles I and Parliament, is the seventeenth-century basket hilted broadsword, with a straight two-edged blade, it was the favourite weapon of the cavalry (plate 7). Where the blade has only one cutting edge it is known as a backsword. The English basket hilt has a large rounded pommel which distinguishes it from the Scottish basket hilt with its flattened conical pommel.

From the sixteenth century the pistol has rivalled the sword for pride of place as a personal weapon and was carried in time of war as a complementary arm to the sword.

From the time of the earliest wheel-lock pistols they have had

8

Plate 2
Spanish cup-hilted rapier, early 17th century. The double edged blade signed
xx EN xx MENE xx.

9

Plate 3
Italian left hand dagger with sheath, late
16th century. The hilt and sheath mounts
decorated with silver studs. The blade
pierced through in the grooves.

10

a particular fascination, and there is no doubt that they are the most popular of collected weapons. A case is recorded of a young gentleman, in the sixteenth century, who accidentally wounded his mistress with an early wheel-lock pistol while he was playing with it instead of giving attention to the rival attractions of his lady.

The wheel-lock pistols of the sixteenth century had intricate mechanisms that were costly to produce, the ignition being by means of a spinning serrated wheel striking sparks into the priming pan, from a piece of iron pyrites held in place in the jaws of the dog head.

Many of the sixteenth century wheel-lock pistols were of German manufacture, of a curious elongated triangular shape with a ball-shaped end to the butt, all profusely inlaid with stagshorn on which were engraved a variety of foliated designs, birds, animals of the chase and classical motifs. These pistols are of course very rare and when they do appear in sale-rooms they fetch very high prices.

The seventeenth century saw ignition by means of flint and steel: first the snaphaunce and later the flintlock proper in which the steel and flashpan cover were combined. Flintlock ignition was to reign supreme for two hundred years until finally dethroned by percussion ignition in the early years of the nineteenth century.

The elegant long-barrelled wheel-lock holster pistols of the early seventeenth century are also rare but the plainer ones may be within the reach of some collectors. Similar long-barrelled pistols followed, first of snaphaunce and then flint-lock which were a normal part of the equipment of seventeenth-century cavalry, carried in the holsters on either side of the saddle. The best of these seventeenth century pistols are amongst the most graceful and elegantly enriched of all. The long barrels are often chiselled, engraved or inlaid and the locks, sideplates and furniture likewise. Many of the woods used to stock these pistols have a grain which is exotically figured, and some are also carved (plates 8 and 9).

A very few early seventeenth century English pistols are to be found with the original English flintlock usually named the dog-lock because of the dog catch that secures it at half-cock. This was the earliest form of flintlock in which the steel and

11

flash pan cover were combined and because of its early intro-duction the snaphaunce lock, though not entirely unknown, is extremely rare in English guns.

By the mid-seventeenth century the French type of flintlock had been adopted in England and of particular interest are the very fine rifled pistols with turn off barrels. These were loaded at the breech, by first unscrewing the barrel. The powder load was put into the breech and a ball rested on the rounded recess in the top of the breech; then the barrel was screwed on again. Next the cock holding the flint being safe at half-cock the pan was primed and the steel and pan cover or frizzen pulled back to hold the priming in place. In this manner the pistol was carried loaded; the cock had only to be raised to full-cock and the pistol was ready to fire. For the reason that lay behind this turn-off style of loading it must be understood that the problem at this time was to get sufficient velocity from a relatively slow burning gunpowder to penetrate a breastplate. The long barrels of the seventeenth century holster pistols were one answer, but the turn-off system had the advantage that a tight fitting ball could be loaded from the breech, giving a gas-tight fit and keying tightly into the rifling, ensuring that use was made of the full force of the powder. These pistols were also very accurate, a story being told of the famous Cavalier general Prince Rupert demonstrating his skill with his rifled pistols to his uncle King Charles I by hitting a steeple-cock with each of his pair of pistols. The disadvantage of these turn-off pistols lay in the difficulty of re-loading in action, and sometimes these pistols are to be found with ramrods added so that after the first discharge they could be re-loaded with a smaller patched ball from the muzzle (plate 10).

Plate 4
Left: French smallsword, late 17th century. The steel hilt chiselled with human figures against a gilt ground. The blade blued and gilt with engraved decorations.
Centre: French smallsword, third quarter of 17th cen-tury, steel hilt damascened with gold decoration.
Right: French smallsword, late 18th century. Hilt steel with pierced and gilt decoration. Blade blued and gilt with etched designs.

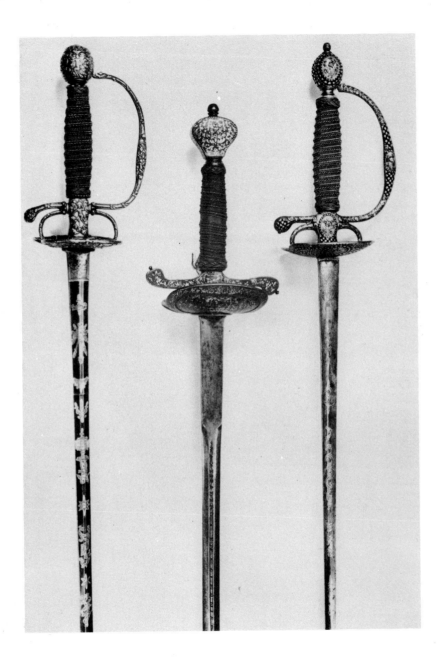

13

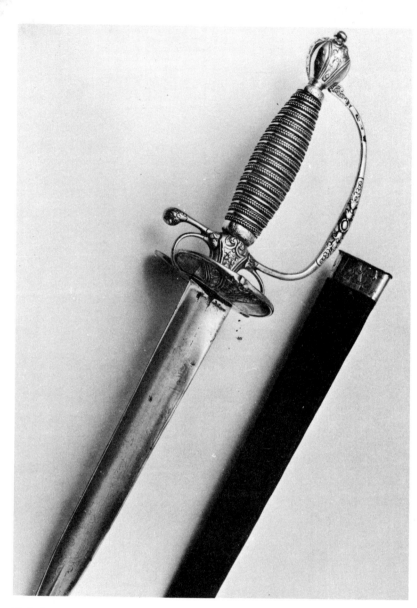

Plate 5
English silver hilted smallsword and scabbard. London Hall mark for 1750, maker's name John Carmen. Colichmarde blade.

This turn-off type of pistol remained popular through the eighteenth century (plate 11) and part of the nineteenth century as a pocket pistol. These include the most attractive cannon-barrelled pistols with silver wire inlay and silver mask-head butt plates (plate 12). The early eighteenth century pistols of this type had side-locks but the later ones are mostly box-locks, that is the cock and frizzen are set in a central position behind the breech; this made them more narrow and therefore more convenient for carrying in a pocket (plate 13). The cock in the centre of course prevented accurate aiming but then these personal protection weapons were designed for use at very close range. Later some pocket pistols were fitted with short, spring-out daggers, released by a sliding trigger guard.

Eighteenth century pistols were for the most part smooth bore muzzle-loaders, the typical holster pistol resembled earlier types but had a shorter barrel. It was customary for most pistols to be made in pairs; this idea probably originated in holster pistols being carried on either side of the saddle and the custom was continued for other sorts of pistol. There was however in the second half of the eighteenth century an important type of pistol which was of necessity made as a matched pair. These pistols were designed specially for settling affairs of honour and are generally known as duelling pistols. Duelling, though illegal in Britain, was nevertheless fairly common in the eighteenth and first half of the nineteenth century. In earlier duels the small sword had been used, but as this gave a considerable advantage to the party skilled in the art of fencing, the pistol eventually became the established arbiter of such disputes, there being more element of chance.

At first any suitable pair of pistols was used but in the second half of the eighteenth century a distinct type of duelling pistol was evolved. The general practice in duels with pistols was for the aggrieved parties to stand back to back, pistol pointed to the ground, walk an agreed number of paces, turn, and on the word fire the arm was raised and the pistol fired without taking deliberate aim. Now it was this point of not taking a deliberate aim that inspired the gunmaker Robert Wogdon to develop a pistol, which when raised, became a natural extension of the arm and pointed directly at the mark that the eye looked at. No doubt Wogdon was trying to be helpful, but the effect must

15

have been to put up the casualty rate. However this may have been, the duelling pistol generally evolved into one having a nine or ten inch octagonal barrel, smooth bored of about twenty-eight gauge (twenty-eight balls to the pound) and full stocked (the wood of the stock coming up to the end of the barrel). The main difference was in the butt, the bulbous ended butt and butt plate of the typical holster pistol was discarded in favour of a plain wood butt that curved round towards the trigger guard and was finished with a flat on either side (plate 14). The locks of duelling pistols are, as would be expected, of excellent quality, for a misfire was most undesirable in the circumstances. Apart from Wogdon fine duelling pistols were made by such gunmakers as Twigg, Mortimer and Egg. Around 1800 the famous Manton brothers John and Joseph produced some very workmanlike duelling pistols, half-stocked with checkered rounded butt, heavy octagonal barrels, superbly finished locks and set triggers (plate 15). These set triggers, also used on rifles of the period, enabled the pistol to be fired by the lightest touch of the finger thus avoiding the common fault of pulling off the point of aim when pulling the trigger. The set trigger was cocked by pressing the rear of the trigger forward until the sear of the set trigger spring was lightly caught, and then on the slightest touch of the trigger it flicked up to release the main lock sear. The action was so light that a small member called a detent was added to the lock to ride the sear over the half-cock bent.

These set triggers are adjustable by means of a small screw behind the trigger and are a good example of the highly skilled work that went into a top quality pistol, that is out of sight. The essence of English gunmaking in the late eighteenth century and nineteenth century was concentration on the efficiency and finish of the essential parts of the gun, the plain but gracefully proportioned overall shape being enriched only by the unobtrusive engraving of the locks and iron furniture.

In fact these set triggers were rather tricky to use in a duel because a nervous person could easily fire the pistol prematurely. Probably because of the possible need, gentlemen took to practising pistol shooting at targets and it was in target practice, that later became popular for its own sake, that the set trigger was a considerable asset. Several London gunmakers set up

16

Plate 6
English silver hilted smallsword. London
Hall mark for 1750. Blade of colichmarde
type.

17

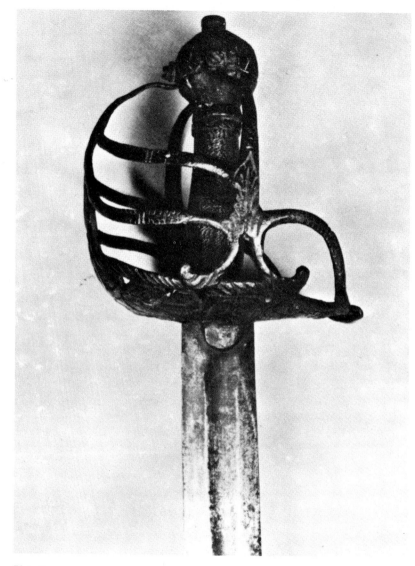

Plate 7
English broadsword, mid 17th century.
Iron hilt decorated with foliage and masks.
Blade bears the 'running wolf' mark.
Typical cavalry sword of English Civil
War.

18

shooting galleries, amongst the first being Joseph Lang whose gallery was opened in 1827 in the Haymarket. James Purdey made some of the finest of the later duelling pistols, both flint and percussion cap.

Pistol shooting with duelling pistols was later followed by shooting with distinctive target pistols of the overall size of duelling pistols but rifled and accurately sighted. Duelling pistols exist which have very shallow rifling and some have the first inch or two bored smooth to hide the rifling.

There were occasions when rifled pistols were used for duels but such instances were rare. A case was in fact brought before the House of Lords in which the surviving Peer was charged with murder because rifled pistols had been used, but it was held that, both pistols being rifled, he had no unfair advantage.

Some curious duels are recorded in the 'Annals of Sporting' of 1822 among the sporting occurrences for each month. In May the Duke of Bedford and the Duke of Buckingham, in a dispute about derogatory remarks allegedly made, met in Kensington Gardens: they fired at twelve paces without effect but as Bedford shot in the air Buckingham came forward saying that in view of this the matter could go no further and they quickly made up the quarrel and parted friends. In each of two further duels recorded one of the seconds was killed by mistake and in another would have been but for the fact 'that the shot had been omitted as usual'. It seems that in some duels the seconds saw to it that both pistols were loaded with blank charges for the first shot, and if honour was satisfied with no harm done, so much the better, but if the hot-heads insisted on 'tapping the claret' then for the second shot the pistols were loaded with ball. Such was the case in an Irish duel when, after the first discharge had proved ineffective, both men were killed by the second. This use sometimes of blanks for the first round is further borne out by a report of a duel at Chalk Farm between two gamblers, one of whom on the second fire got 'winged' in the pistol arm. The report goes on: 'It is believed their first shots were blanks, since the men took good aim at each other, without doing execution'.

From about the last quarter of the eighteenth century it became the custom for gunmakers to sell pairs of duelling pistols in fine mahogany cases with a brass ring handle or drop

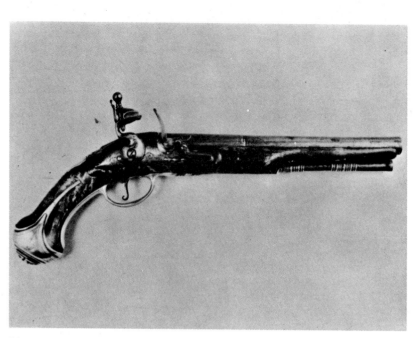

Plate 8
English flintlock holster pistol by Thomas
Green *circa* 1690. Finely figured stock and
mounts of engraved brass.

handle on the lid, green baize lined compartments and their
engraved trade label on the inside of the lid. Prior to this pistols
were sold in covers of thick blanket material. With the pistols
were also compartments for the powder flask, bullet mould,
loading and cleaning rod, turnscrews, spare flints, and flint
leathers. Additional items could be a patch cutter, loading rod,
mallet and starter. Many pistols were from this time sold cased,
and to a collector they are most desirable in this form especially
if all is in original condition including all the fittings (colour
plate 1).

A useful pointer to the approximate date of pistols in the
nineteenth century is the use of platinum for touch holes in
place of gold between 1805 and 1810. The locks between then
and 1820 will show the latest improvements to the flintlock:
rainproof pans of 'V' or narrow oval shape, short strong cocks

Colour plate 5   20
Blunderbuss and flask.

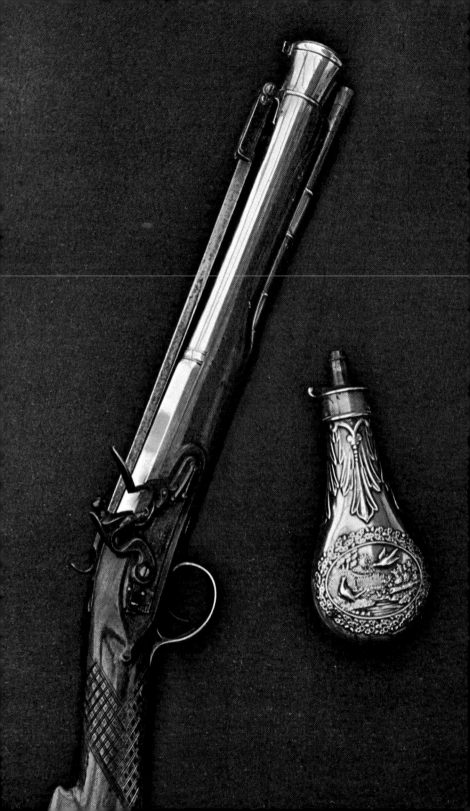

for quick firing, of the French or spur type (plate 16) or the double necked cock.

In the early years of the nineteenth century when the flint-lock, after some two hundred years, was reaching its last stages of perfection, a rival form of ignition challenged it. The new form of ignition was by means of a detonating powder invented by the Reverend Forsyth who patented the system in 1807. At first Forsyth used a rather complicated system involving a small magazine of detonating powder, usually named the 'scent bottle,' but in the course of a few years various systems were evolved by a number of leading gunmakers in which the detonating powder was contained in pills, discs, tubes, tapes and caps. By the early 1820s the copper cap with the detona-

Plate 9
French flintlock holster pistols by Frenel of Paris, early 18th century. The name in gold on blued barrels, walnut stocks, engraved steel furniture.

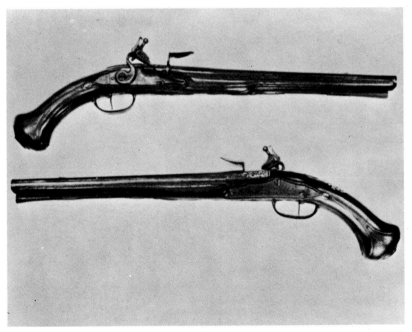

Colour plate 6
Target pistols, J. Purdey.

21

ting mixture inside, placed on a hollow cone-shaped nozzle (usually referred to as the 'nipple') and fired by a hammer, had become the most widely applied means of percussion ignition. With percussion ignition a misfire was unlikely and also because it was quicker than the fastest flint it was an aid to accurate shooting.

A variety of pistols, from duelling to pocket pistols, were converted to percussion cap ignition, the usual method being by means of a plug screwed into the position of the touch-hole,

Plate 10
Pair of English flintlock turn-off pocket pistols by E. Gifford, late 17th century. Engraved with strawberry foliage.

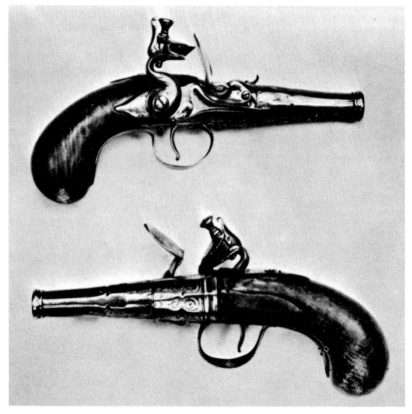

Plate 11
Pair of English flintlock turn-off, cannon barrelled pistols by T. Davis of London, *circa* 1750. Grotesque mask butt-cap, escutcheon and sideplate in silver.

removal of the frizzen and pan, and the substituting of a percussion hammer for the flint cock. A superior method involved the fitting of a new breech and new percussion lock; this was much more expensive but infinitely more satisfactory, giving quicker and stronger shooting.

Some of the side plug conversions have in recent years been converted back to their original flint form of ignition, due to the fact that fine flint pistols usually fetch much higher prices than percussion conversions, especially by the cheaper method. There are a number of specialists who are skilled in filing up parts for antique guns and some are capable of making parts comparable with the originals.

23

From early times in the history of pistols there had been many ideas for increasing the number of shots that a pistol could fire. The superimposed load system was used to a limited extent with a lock that slid back to line up one after the other with the touch holes. Two locks were used in wheel-lock pistols. Double barrelled flintlock pistols were, in the first instance, mostly on the over and under principle, turning over to bring the under barrel and its frizzen to the single cock. Most of the eighteenth and nineteenth century double barrelled pistols were of the side by side type with a lock on either side. In the early nineteenth century Joseph Egg produced some of the finest little double barrelled pistols ever made (colour plate 2). These little pocket pistols had double barrels on the over and under principle, and a pair of locks operated by a single trigger. The neat and narrow look of these pistols is achieved by using an external mainspring which also serves the frizzen and is linked by a swivel to a toe projecting from the lower part of the spur cock.

The idea of using an external mainspring may have been inspired by the Spanish flintlock or Miquelet lock with its upright cock and external mainspring.

Joseph, like his famous uncle, Durs Egg, had his name inlaid in gold on the top of the barrel of most of his best pistols and guns. The butt plates and trigger guards are usually in silver but some are in gold, for instance those he made for the Prince Regent (later George IV) who was an enthusiastic collector and shooter of fine guns.

Once at a dinner in Brighton in 1805 he invited the guests to see him shoot with an air gun at a target set at the end of the room; he shot very well but when he insisted that the ladies present had a try, the ceiling, a door and a fiddler were hit.

Some heavy calibre officers' pistols of the over and under kind were also made in the early nineteenth century, the barrels being of octagonal section and the locks set on either side having normal internal mainsprings. Finely finished examples of this type were made by John Manton amongst others (plates 17 and 18).

The revolver principle had been applied to pistols in the seventeenth century, using a snaphaunce lock and chambers turned by hand. In 1818 Elisha Collier, an American from

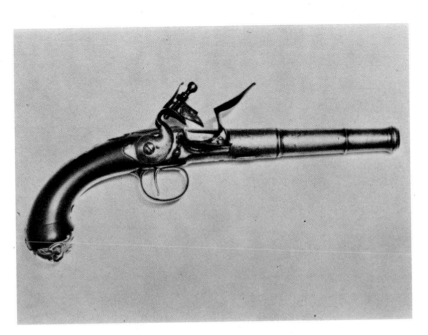

Plate 12
English flintlock turn-off cannon barrelled
pistol by J. Freeman, London, *circa* 1750.
The escutcheon, sideplate and butt mask
in silver.

Boston, brought to England his ingenious flintlock revolver and
later he set up in business in the Strand, London. This Collier
revolver needed only to be re-cocked and the frizzen pulled
back for the pistol to be ready to fire again. This was accom-
plished by means of a complicated system of springs which
moved the next chamber in line with the barrel, and forward
into the cone shaped chamber recess, which formed a gas-tight
fit into the barrel end. At the same time the frizzen, embodying
a magazine of priming powder, automatically primed the pan
on being pulled back into its firing position.

A few revolving multi-barrelled flint pistols were made, of
the type usually known by the amusing name of 'pepperboxes'.
Flintlock revolvers and pepperboxes are rare and naturally
fetch high prices, but the percussion cap types which followed
them in great numbers and variety provide plenty of scope for

25

Plate 13
One of a pair of English turn-off flintlock
pocket pistols by R. Noyes Junior of
Warminster *circa* 1800. Brass frames, silver
inlay on butt.

a specialised collection, though the increased interest in them has already been reflected in rapidly rising prices.

Between about the late 1820s and the 1840s these percussion pepperboxes were manufactured in large numbers, particularly in England, France and Belgium. They were made in many different designs, with overhead, side or internal hammers. In some the hammer was cocked to bring the barrel into line, but most are double action, the trigger-pull both cocking and releasing the hammer and also bringing the next barrel into line (plate 19).

Pepperboxes could be described as something of ugly ducklings among pistols, but they are certainly very businesslike and no doubt facing the multiple barrel ends must have had a deterrent affect upon those at whom they were pointed. There are however exceptions to the purely functional models; these are to be found finely finished, enriched with engraved silver and set snugly in their velvet lined cases surrounded by good quality fittings such as: the bullet mould, nipple key, powder flask, cleaning rod, spare nipples and a tin of percussion caps (plate 20). Such complete sets are most desirable, not least because they provide the collector with interesting clues as to the intended load, size and shape of the percussion cap, shape of an unused nipple and size of the hole in it, size of the ball and the thickness of the patch used. There may also be instructions for loading in the lid of the case, and where the silver mounts are hall marked, the exact date can soon be found and of course the name of the silversmith. Silversmiths would usually carry out work for the gun trade but were not as a rule directly employed by gunmakers (colour plate 4).

For the collector who wishes to expand from pepperboxes alone there is a further group of pistols sometimes called transitional revolvers which are rather like pepperboxes with short barrels or chambers, to which a single revolver type barrel has been added (plates 21 and 22). These mostly still retain the typical over-head hammer of the pepperbox type which hits the percussion cap and nipple at right angles to the chamber. Later, around the 1850s when pinfire cartridges arrived on the scene, a cheap pinfire pepperbox with a folding trigger was popular in France and Belgium.

Although American weapons will be dealt with in a later

chapter, it is necessary at this stage to mention the arrival in England of Samuel Colt in 1851 to show his revolvers at the Great Exhibition. As a result he received large orders for his Navy pattern Colt (colour plate 16) from the British Government which encouraged him to open a factory at Millbank, London. The action of the British Government in buying Colt's revolvers spurred British gunmakers into action to provide rival revolvers.

The Colt revolver had to be cocked by the thumb before each shot; because such an action was necessary in order to shoot with accuracy at long range, this was not an important handicap in the open warfare conditions of the American frontier. However in close hand to hand fighting such as occurred in the Crimea and the Indian Mutiny or in boarding a ship at sea, the double action revolver, that cocked and fired

Plate 14
Fine pair of silver mounted duelling pistols by Robert Wogdon, London Hall mark for 1774.

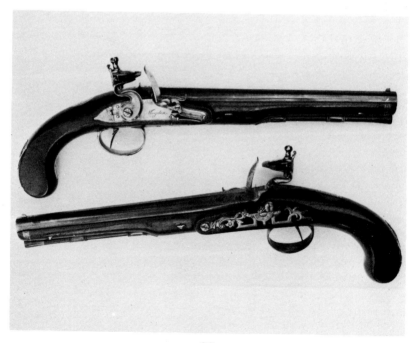

28

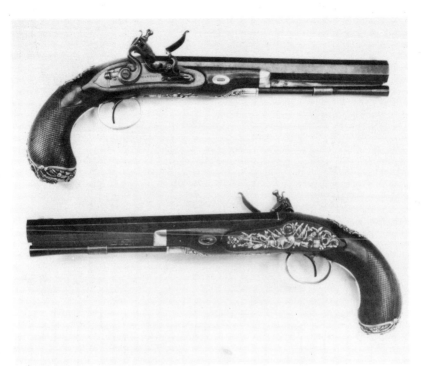

Plate 15
Pair of silver mounted flintlock presentation duelling pistols by John Manton,
London, *circa* 1810. Manton inlaid in
gold on the octagonal browned twist
barrels, gold touch-holes and foresights.
Half stocked, with chequered butts.

with the one pull of the trigger, was generally favoured for
these conditions.

Many well constructed and finely finished British revolvers
were produced by such gunmakers as Tranter (plate 23),
Westley Richards, Adams and Webley (plate 24). Unlike the
Colts, the solid frame was mostly used, that is with a connection
over the chambers. It was the sturdy and well designed Adams
pattern that was adopted as the official service arm in 1855. A
characteristic of many of the British revolvers is the projection
above the hand grip which recalls the saw handled duelling
pistols of the Regency period.

29

Unlike the average pepperbox, these percussion revolvers have very good overall lines and proportions, they are a delight to handle. They are only now beginning to fetch the sort of prices they deserve in relation to Colts, which have for some time fetched much higher prices. Fine percussion revolvers were usually sold in oak cases with compartments for such items as the bullet mould, nipple key, turnscrew, powder flask, a spare set of nipples, oil bottle, cleaning rod, a tin of bullet lubricant, a wad cutter and caps. In addition to the trade label in the lid, there are sometimes instructions for use as well. Such cased sets are most attractive, but if a collector has limited means he has to decide whether to collect a quantity of uncased revolvers as examples of different types or save up and buy only fine cased examples. Quantity or quality is the eternal dilemma in collecting, but where appreciation in value is concerned, quality and fine condition are usually the winners.

Some officers on service in India preferred heavy calibre double barrelled pistols to revolvers because of their great stopping power and straight forward mechanism. These pistols were also useful on shikar as a secondary weapon to be used on dangerous animals, and were continued as 'howdah' pistols with pinfire and later centre fire cartridges. Charles Lancaster's four barrelled centre fire pistol was also popular.

Fine rifled target pistols were made in the percussion period and these are particularly desirable because of their quality and the fact that the cased pairs are often lavishly equipped (plate 25). Typical of the French and Belgian kind are those in Gothic style (plate 26), deeply carved all over with Gothic fantasies, the fittings are similarly enriched, laid out in snug fitting compartments of velvet or gold tooled leather. The British target pistols on the other hand are elegant in shape and

Plate 16
Fine pair of flintlock presentation pistols by Bennett and Lacy, London. Silver mounts with Birmingham hall mark for 1811. Barrels blued with etched and gilt decoration. Lock with French or spur cocks. Typical of richly ornate pistols designed for presentation to Oriental princes.

31

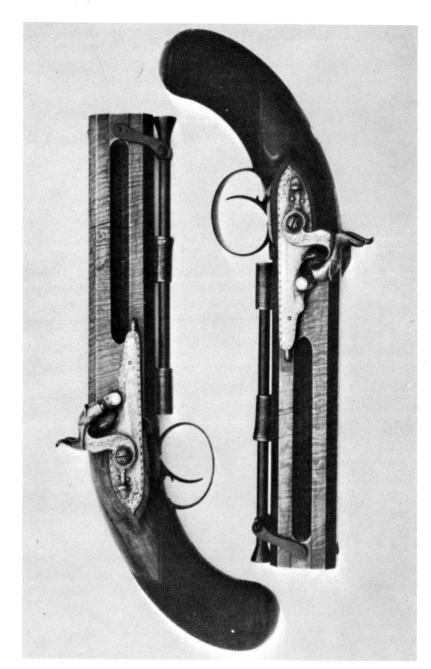

restrained in enrichment, relying on fine scroll engraving only. Good examples were made by several leading gunmakers including James Purdey (colour plate 6) who was better known for fine sporting guns and rifles; the author has shot with examples of these and can vouch for their accuracy, handling qualities and superb finish. These provide yet another example of a quality pistol in which the best work is out of sight: in the rifling of the barrel, the inside of the lock and in the set trigger mechanism.

The blunderbuss has always caught the attention of collectors and the general public. There is something about its great bell-mouthed brass barrel that immediately attracts attention. It has been and remains a most popular weapon, interesting in its historic associations as it is decorative when hung in its traditional place over the fireplace. There were sound reasons for its place over the fire when it was in its heyday as a self-protection weapon, for as the blunderbuss had to be kept charged and primed if it was to be ready for use, it was essential that it be kept where both the main charge and the priming would remain dry. Incidentally, because they were often left loaded for long periods, they may in some instances be found to be still loaded. The author once flashed powder in the pan of a newly acquired blunderbuss, trying the lock, and was somewhat surprised when the congealed mixture of corroded brass and old gunpowder in the breech fizzed off like a firework. It is just as well to remember that gunpowder left in an old flask for a hundred years or more may be almost as powerful as it was when made; so treat it with caution and do not smoke when examining it, for a flask full of old black powder could explode with tremendous force.

The blunderbuss, firing a load of swan or goose shot, was a popular self-protection, military and naval weapon in most parts of Europe in the seventeenth century. It appeared in

Plate 17
Pair of over and under officers' pistols by John Manton and Sons, *circa* 1812. Converted from flintlock to percussion ignition at a later date.

33

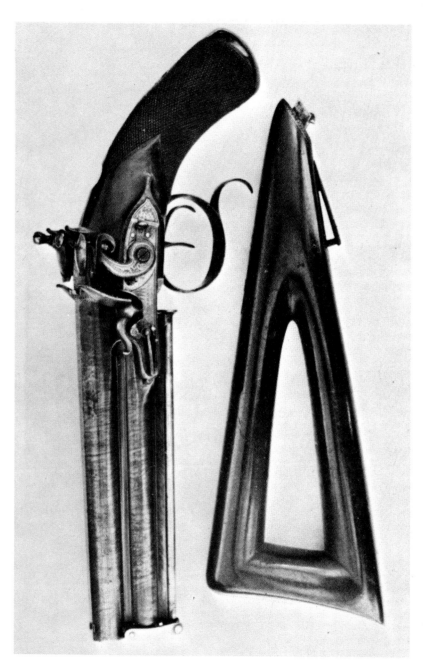

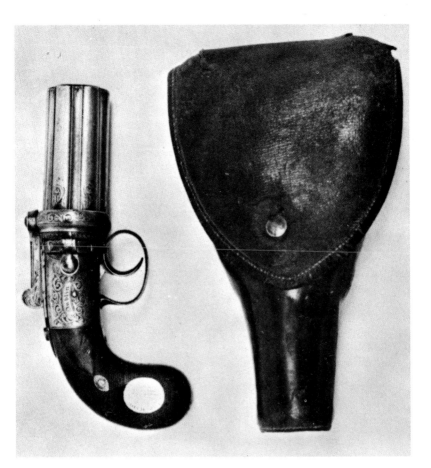

Plate 19
Six barrelled pepperbox pistol by W. & J.
Rigby of Dublin, with original holster. The
silver escutcheon records that the pistol
belonged to Captain Wade of the 90th
Light Infantry who carried this pistol
throughout the Crimean War and Indian
Mutiny.

Plate 18
Officers' double barrelled over and under
pistol by Staudenmayer London, *circa* 1810,
with carbine stock. Spur cocks, rainproof
pans, swivel ramrod.

Plate 20
Fine J. R. Cooper's patent pepperbox
pistol retailed by J. Liversidge of Gains-
borough, *circa* 1845. Original condition, in
its case with all accessories.

Britain around the middle of that century fired by means of the
English dog-lock. The brass barrels, of differing lengths, were
finished with slight to moderate bell-mouths, round the ends
of which were sometimes engraved the warning legend:
'HAPPY IS HE THAT ESCAPETH ME'. The heel plate,
trigger guard, ramrod pipes and so on were usually of brass;
this use of brass may have originated in the use of blunderbusses at sea for boarding and repelling boarders, or because
they were carried in all sorts of weather on coaches. Whether
this was the reason or not, iron barrelled versions are much less
common but because they are less attractive generally they
fetch lower prices.

In the latter part of the seventeenth century and the eighteenth century the French type of flintlock was used though the overall shape remained much the same. However, towards the end of the eighteenth and early nineteenth century the barrel took on a generally shorter length with octagonal moulding at the breech end and heavily moulded rings and bell-mouth at the muzzle. This type was typical of those specifically made for coach guards for protection from highwaymen. They were often fitted with a triangular bayonet that sprang over and locked, on pulling back the thumb lever behind the breech (colour plate 5). The Birmingham firm of Ketland made large quantities of blunderbusses and those by Henry Nock are highly regarded.

Before leaving the subject of blunderbusses it would be well to clear up two popular falacies about them. Firstly they were not normally loaded with a whole lot of odd bits and pieces because these would not be thrown in as evenly spread a pattern as would shot of a standard size. Secondly the shot does not leave the barrel in the width of arc suggested by the bell-mouth; in fact it leaves with much the same spread as it would from a cylinder barrel of the same length. The big bell muzzle

Plate 21
Six chambered transitional revolver with Birmingham proof marks and the name Nock London on the frame. *Circa* 1850.

Colour plate 8
Charge of Scots Greys.

37

had, however, a considerable deterrent value, for the beholder must have felt that there was no escaping the fire from that awesome barrel.

A number of brass barrelled blunderbuss pistols were made as self-protection and coaching weapons and some of these were also fitted with small spring bayonets.

In several parts of Europe distinctive types of weapons were evolved and of particular interest are those of Scotland associated as they are with the romance of the Highlands, clan feuds, the rebellions of 1715 and 45 and Prince Charles Edward Stuart.

Plate 22
Baker's Patent transitional revolver *circa* 1852. The long spurred hammer stamped Baker's patent. Nickel frame.

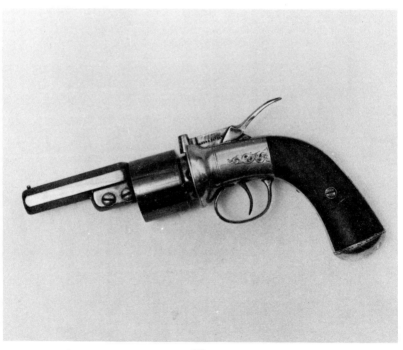

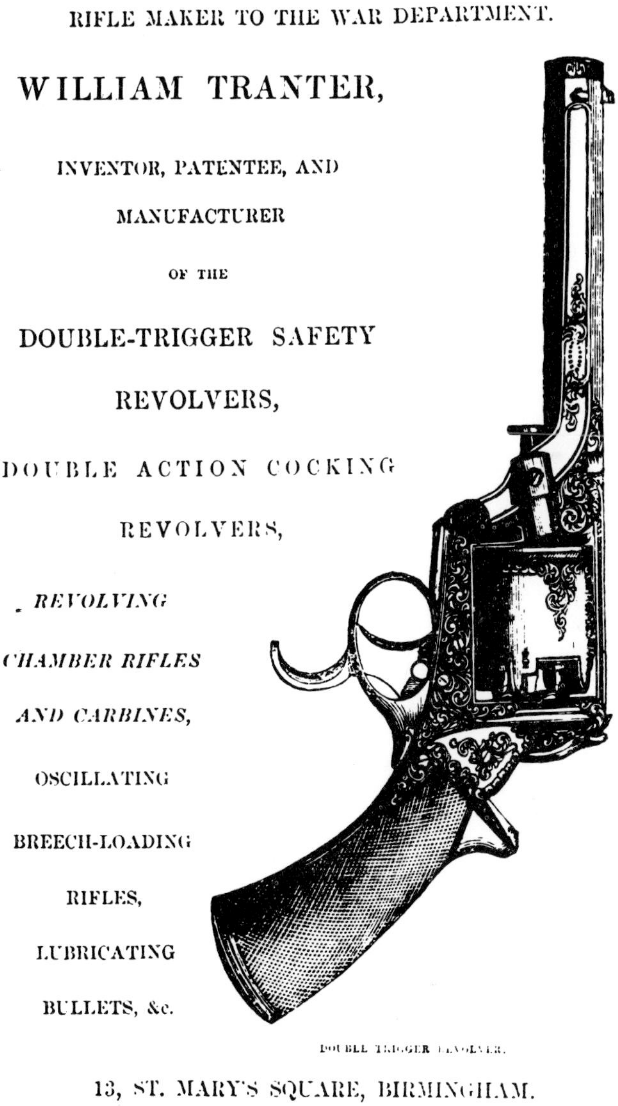

RIFLE MAKER TO THE WAR DEPARTMENT.

WILLIAM TRANTER,

INVENTOR, PATENTEE, AND

MANUFACTURER

OF THE

DOUBLE-TRIGGER SAFETY

REVOLVERS,

DOUBLE ACTION COCKING

REVOLVERS,

REVOLVING

CHAMBER RIFLES

AND CARBINES,

OSCILLATING

BREECH-LOADING

RIFLES,

LUBRICATING

BULLETS, &c.

DOUBLE TRIGGER REVOLVER.

13, ST. MARY'S SQUARE, BIRMINGHAM.

Plate 23
William Tranter's percussion revolver.
Woodcut advertisement 1858.

39

PHILIP WEBLEY,

84, WEAMAN STREET, BIRMINGHAM,

PRESENT CONTRACTOR TO THE HON. BOARD OF ORDNANCE,

PATENTEE OF SAFETY REVOLVING PISTOLS.

P. WEBLEY respectfully informs the public, that he is prepared to supply in any quantity his

PATENT REVOLVING PISTOLS,

Plate 24
Philip Webley's percussion revolver. Wood
cut advertisement 1858.

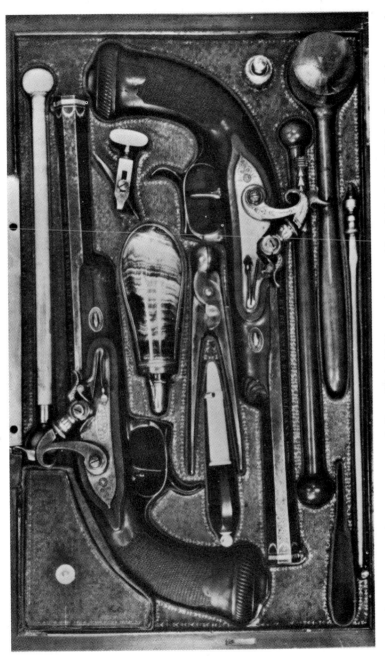

Plate 25 Fine pair of pellet lock target pistols by Le Page of Paris. Multi-grooved octagonal barrels blued with gold inlay. Spurred trigger-guards and set triggers. Gold tooled red morocco leather lined case. Mid 1820s.

41

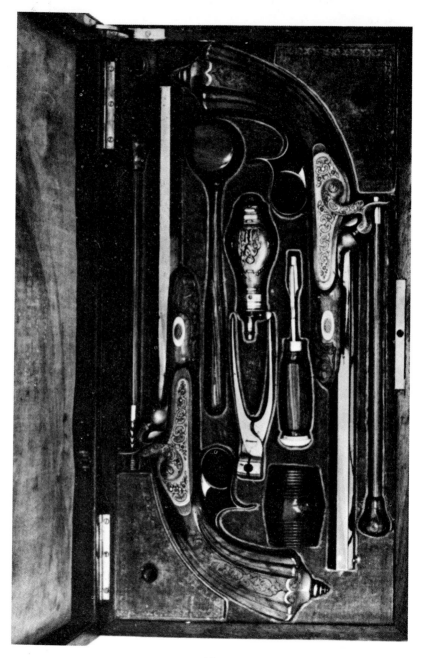

In early times distinctive weapons were the true claymore, a great two handed sword with straight double-edged blade and the Lochaber axe, a great long bladed pole axe. However, in the seventeenth and eighteenth centuries, the typical Highlander was armed with a basket hilted broadsword or backsword, a long bladed dirk at his waist, a skean dhu (small broad bladed dagger) (plate 27) in his stocking and a pair of all-steel belt pistols. In war he might also carry a gun or a round shield (targe) made from wood covered with leather and studded with brass nails (colour plate 7). All these are most desirable collectors' items, especially when they are of fine quality. The Scottish broadswords or backswords have fine springy steel blades, mostly imported from Germany and bearing the 'trade mark' Andrea Ferrara. The early dirks have long, broad, single-edged blades, double-edged towards the sharp point. The flatish hilt is of wood carved in a series of interlaced patterns, the top being finished with a circular brass or silver disc, decorated with designs of celtic origin, which secures the tang. Pockets in the leather scabbard were provided for a small knife and fork. In the nineteenth century these dirks became very ornate, enriched with engraved silver, with cairngorms mounted in the top of the hilt and also in the top of the knife and fork handles.

Scottish belt pistols have many interesting features and fine examples are much sought after. Seventeenth century pistols have the Scottish version of the snaphaunce lock, the early type having a wooden stock finished with the so called fishtail butt with a metal butt plate. Other distinctive features are the small baluster trigger, without a guard, the long belt hook and the fact that some of these were made with right and left handed locks, presumably so that a pistol could be drawn easily from the belt by the left or right hand as required. Also in the seventeenth century came the all metal pistols, firstly stocked

Plate 26
Pair of percussion target or duelling pistols
by Le Page of Paris, mid 19th century. In
the modified Gothic style. Velvet lined case.

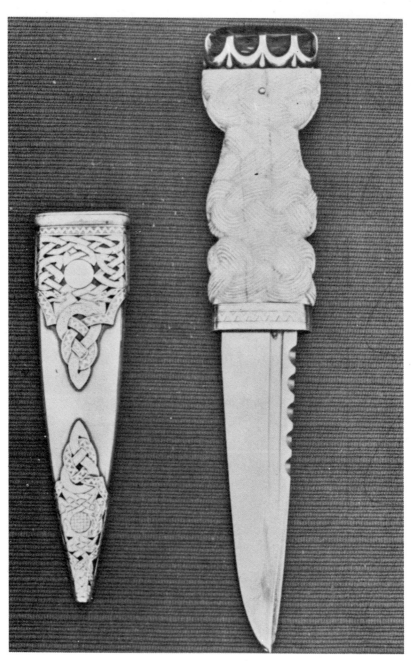

44

in brass and later all steel. The fish tail was replaced in the earlier all metal pistols by a heart shaped butt and later, by the most common, the flat-sided butt finished in two curled steel tendrils with the knob of the pricker (for cleaning the touch hole) between; this type is usually referred to as a ram's horn butt (plate 28).

By 1700 the typical later Scottish pistol, which had adopted the flintlock with the combined steel and pan cover, was rather

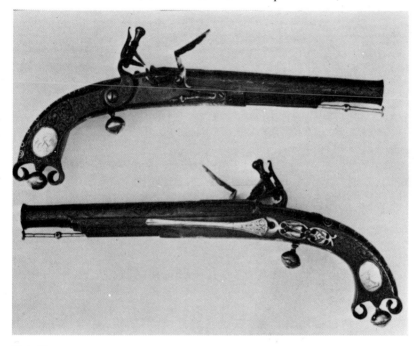

Plate 28
Fine pair of Scottish all steel flintlock pistols by John Campbell, *circa* 1750. The iron stocks engraved with scrolls and inlaid with silver. Ram's horn butt. Silver escutcheons, belt hooks, triggers and pricker heads.

Plate 27
Skean dhu. Victorian silver mounted with a cairngorm, with carved ivory grip.

45

shorter in length and was richly decorated with engraved and inlaid designs of celtic origin. The ball trigger without a guard was retained and pairs continued to be made with right and left handed locks through the eighteenth and into the nineteenth century. The gunmakers of Doune near Perth, for example, John Murdoch, Cadell and Christie, are particularly noted for fine pistols but other fine ones were also made by gunmakers in Edinburgh, Stirling and Leith. The nineteenth-century romanticising of Scottish history led to the production of large numbers of decorative rather than functional pistols, made to be worn with extravagant Highland costumes. The seventeenth-century Scottish long guns have curiously curved and fluted butts, large snaphaunce locks and a ball trigger (examples do exist with trigger guards) but all the guns of this type are very rare.

Of interest are the typical seventeenth-century Scottish powder horns made from cow horn flattened at the sides and decorated with scratched or cut designs of a geometric type.

Though some of these personal weapons were from time to time used in warfare, the following chapter will deal with the weapons specifically designed and approved by the government for issue to the armed forces.

2. Military and naval weapons

Military and Naval weapons may be described as standard service arms ordered by the appropriate government department to be made to an approved specification. In Britain the department concerned with the design and ordering of weapons for the armed forces was the Board of Ordnance.

The collector of Military weapons has a very wide field open to him, so for this reason he will probably wish to specialise to some extent. There are for instance: particularly interesting periods of military history, various classes of weapon such as swords, pistols, muskets, rifles and bayonets, or a collector may concentrate on the history of a particular regiment. Whether interest in the weapons or military history comes first, they will soon become inseparately linked. In this brief introduction to the vast subject of military arms a few interesting periods and the weapons associated with them will be outlined.

The English Civil War 1642–1651 fought between the supporters of Charles I and those of Parliament, stirred the imagination of writers and artists in the nineteenth century, and has recently attracted numerous enthusiasts devoted to refighting the Civil War battles on their original sites, costumed and armed appropriately.

The outstanding Royalist cavalry commander, dashing Prince Rupert of the Rhine, had already adopted the Swedish tactics of charging sword in hand to carry the full momentum through the enemy ranks. Their pistols were used in the mêlée and as skirmishing weapons. To counter the Royalist cavalry Oliver Cromwell in the winter of 1642–3 raised a cavalry regiment in his native East Anglia from good quality recruits well armed with a broadsword (plate 7), carbine and a pair of pistols. They wore a buff leather coat, breast and back plates and a helmet with peak, face bars, 'lobster tail' neck guard and ear pieces.

The test of these 'Ironsides' came at Marston Moor, 1644, when they stood firm after Prince Rupert's cavalry had swept most of Parliament's forces from the field; but carrying the pursuit too far they gave Cromwell his chance. Advancing at a steady trot his Ironsides rolled up the flank of the unprotected Royalist infantry and won the day.

Following the success of Cromwell's cavalry, further regiments were raised on similar lines forming the basis of the New Model Army. To the cavalry were added dragoons equipped with musket and sword and infantry with flintlock muskets (of the English dog-lock type), supported by a third of their number with pikes. These musketeers wore red coats which were to remain in one form or another until the late nineteenth century.

The weapons of the New Model Army were probably the nearest an English Army had come to a standardised issue, but they were still ordered from a variety of sources. Orders for basket hilted broadswords, for instance, were put out to various cutlers at a price around 4s. 6d. each, to be fitted with continental blades.

Authentic weapons of the type used in the Civil War are fairly rare and it is usually the better quality weapons, such as

Plate 29
Engraving showing Major General Warde and Infantry of the Waterloo period. After a painting by B. Marshall.

49

the rapiers and pistols used by officers, which have tended to survive, rather than the arms of the soldier.

The campaigns of the Duke of Marlborough between 1704 and 1711 are certainly interesting taking in as they do the battle of Blenheim, in which the French were defeated by the combined forces of Marlborough and Prince Eugene, and the victories of Ramillies 1706, Oudenarde 1708 and Malplaquet 1709. The flintlock musket had been fitted with a socket bayonet which rendered the pikemen unnecessary, it also gave increased mobility and effectiveness to the infantry since all were virtually combined pikemen and musketeers. They were drilled to form hollow squares against cavalry and to fire in extended line to exploit their full fire power, about two shots a

Plate 30
Lock of Brown Bess musket, *circa* 1810.
Sling attached to swivel on fore part of the trigger guard.

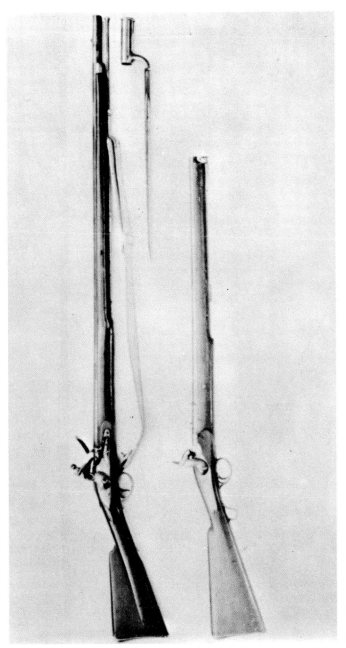

Plate 31

Upper. India pattern Brown Bess musket. 39 inch barrel, lock marked with Crown G.R. and Tower, with buff leather sling and socket bayonet.

Lower. .773 Military percussion carbine with 26 inch barrel. Back action lock marked with Crown, V.R. and Tower 1838. With saddle ring and swivel ramrod.

minute. Each regiment also had grenadiers, chosen from big men for throwing the heavy cast iron grenades.

The really fruitful era for the military collector begins with the Napoleonic Wars, 1792–1815, because of the quantity of arms available, the variety of arms issued to various branches of the army and the increased naming of regiments on arms especially swords. Also this period is fully documented, enabling a collector to gain an intimate knowledge of the development, testing, official approval and use in battle of the arms that interest him.

The Peninsular campaign of the Duke of Wellington and his subsequent victory over Napoleon at Waterloo may well inspire a collector. Landing in Portugal in 1808 with 13,000 men, Sir Arthur Wellesley defeated the French at Vimeiro. He returned in 1809 to command 21,000 men, winning the battles of Oporto and Talavera, then after defeating General Masséna at Mondego, he cautiously retired behind the fortified lines of Torres Vedras for the winter. In March 1811 Massèna retreated and Wellesley regained the Portugese frontier area;

Plate 32
Dragoon pistol marked on lockplate with
Crown, G R and JORDAN 1743.

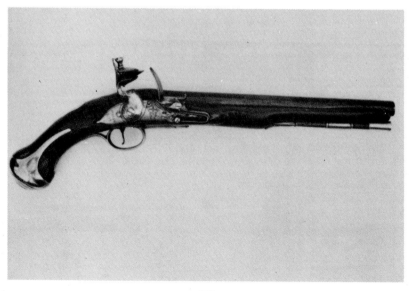

Colour plate 9   52
The 57th.

then followed the two great victories of Salamanca 1812 and Vittoria 1813 which were instrumental in clearing the French from the Peninsula.

Wellesley introduced the self sufficient divisional system and trained his infantry to stand in line to bring to bear the full fire power of their 'Brown Bess' muskets. He would endeavour to draw up his infantry on the reverse side of a ridge, where they were safe from the enemy artillery and out of sight. In front were skirmishers and the flanks were protected by cavalry and mobile horse artillery. The French infantry moving forward in columns saw as they moved over the ridge some 1,000 yards away the long red line before them silent with ordered arms—they moved nearer starting to fire, the red line stood still—they started to run forward but still no movement stirred the ranks ahead. The effect on their morale was dramatic, their ardour cooled, but when only 300 yards away it chilled, as the long red line put their muskets to their shoulders and fired volley after volley decimating the French columns which staggered, faltered and turned. With a great cheer the British infantry charged sweeping their opponents in disorder from the field.

Just when the name Brown Bess was first used for the British musket is uncertain but the first printed reference does not occur until the 1780s. However, the name is now applied by collectors to the series of muskets starting with the New Land Musket introduced in the first quarter of the eighteenth century. This musket had a 46 inch barrel and a wooden ramrod retained by three pipes with a tail pipe where it entered the stock. Brass furniture was used for the heel plate, escutcheon, side plate, trigger guard and ramrod pipes. The lock was also improved and later the wooden ramrod was replaced with an iron rammer. A short Land Musket with a 42 inch barrel was also made, in the first instance, for issue to dragoons and marines, and later to the militia, when these were formed around 1760.

From 1768 the short (42 inch) musket became the standard infantry arm, but on the outbreak of war with France, there being a need for the rapid provision of large numbers of muskets, The Board of Ordnance decided to order large numbers of the type known to collectors as the India pattern

Colour plate 10
Midshipmans' dirks.

53

(plate 30 upper). This musket with a 39 inch barrel, was cheaper and easier to manufacture and had for many years been the standard musket of the army of the East India Company. While the India pattern continued to be made up to 1815, a better quality musket was also made from 1802.

These Brown Bess muskets with their 17 inch triangular socket bayonets would certainly form an important part of a collection of military arms of their period. These muskets were used by the main body of the army in situations which usually called for rapid loading and firing, rather than accuracy. The barrel of 10 bore (·760) was considerably larger than the ball of $14\frac{1}{2}$ bore. It had been 14 but in 1752 it was reduced in size to $14\frac{1}{2}$ bore to make loading easier in a barrel foul from the deposits left by black powder. The ball was not of course loose to rattle about in the bore, for being wrapped round with greased cartridge paper, and having the remainder of the paper which contained the powder charge also rammed down with it, the whole made a sort of combined patch and wad. This gave

Plate 33
Cavalry pistol *circa* 1815 marked on lock-plate with Crown, G R and TOWER. Swivel ramrod and modified butt cap.

54

a reasonable gas-tight fit and stopped the ball rattling loosely from side to side up the bore. The musket gave accuracy up to about 50 yards, moderate shooting at 100 yards and sufficient accuracy for firing into columns of troops at 300 yards.

In addition to muskets numerous carbines were made in various lengths (from 42 to 28 inches) some with provision for bayonets and others without; the common factor being the carbine bore of 17 balls to the pound. These carbines were made principally for issue to light infantry, light dragoons, artillery and the Highland infantry formed in 1757.

Pistols of the type generally known as holster pistols (plate 32) were made, varying in length of barrel from 10 to 12 inches and in bore from 28 bore to carbine or even full musket bore. Late in the eighteenth century 'spurs' or 'ears' on the butt cap that extended up the grip were omitted. Early in the nineteenth century some pistols and carbines were fitted with steel swivel ramrods which had the advantage that they could not be lost in the turmoil of action (plate 33).

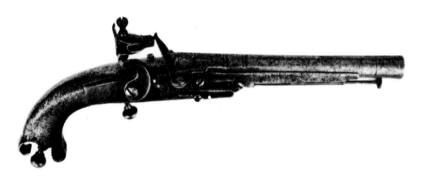

Plate 34
Military Highland pistol by Christie of Doune *circa* 1765. The barrel marked R.H.Regt.

55

Plate 35
The Duke of Richmond's pattern musket
fitted with Henry Nock's screwless enclosed lock. *circa* 1790.

Interesting as curiosities are the Scottish made belt pistols
issued to the newly formed Highland Regiments of Foot (plate
34). Later ones, bearing the name of the Birmingham maker
Isaac Bissell, have the traditional ram's horn butt and belt
hook, but the last model made is of a less pleasing shape with a
flat gun-metal sided butt, lacking the ram's horn tendrils.

The military arms designed by the famous gunmaker Henry
Nock are particularly worthy of attention. In 1783 he designed
a pistol with a detachable butt for the cavalry and in 1793 a
long double barrelled pistol for the Royal Horse Artillery,
which with its detachable stock fitted, became a most useful
double carbine. Nock's screwless enclosed lock brought an
award of £100 from the Ordnance in 1786, and was used for

56

Plate 36
Military Ferguson breech-loading rifle by Durs Egg, *circa* 1780.

57

Plate 37
The Baker rifle, weighing 9½lb and firing
a ball of 20 to the pound.

carbines, pistols and Volunteer rifles. In 1790 he designed the finest musket of its day, known as the Duke of Richmond's pattern, which also was fitted with Nock's patent lock. However after only a few thousand had been produced the project was abandoned because of the difficulties of manufacture and the urgent need for quantity rather than quality on the outbreak of the Napoleonic War.

In this brief outline of the muskets, carbines and pistols used leading up to and during the Napoleonic war, it should be realised that there were many trial weapons and others of limited issue such as carbines of full musket bore and a variety of carbine bayonets. Also in times of urgent need muskets were ordered from continental sources, particularly from the Dutch. For the manufacture of the English muskets, the normal practice was for the Board of Ordnance to order the barrels, locks, furniture etc from contractors, mostly in the Birmingham area, and store these in the Tower Armories. The setting up of the muskets was then put out to London gunmakers specialising in the work under the supervision of officers of the Board of Ordnance.

During the eighteenth century wars in America, first with the French and secondly with the American settlers, the need for accurate rifles had become all too apparent for the skirmishing actions fought in rough country. The need was first filled by ordering rifles from Germany of the type based on the hunting or Jäger rifle.

In 1776 Captain Ferguson patented an improved version of the screw plug type of breech loading rifle (plate 36). His version had a screw plug attached at the base to a forward extension of the trigger guard. To open the breech the trigger guard, acting as a lever, was used to unwind the screw plug one complete turn. The main drawback to this type of action was the liability of the screw to clog, caused by the residue of the black powder. Ferguson endeavoured to minimise this by cutting channels in the plug which helped to keep the fouling clear of the thread. A hundred of these rifles were made in 1776 for the British army and others for the East India Company. In 1877 Captain Ferguson and a detachment of men trained in the use of these rifles set out for America where they distinguished themselves in action. Ferguson however was badly wounded, but on recovery he was appointed Inspector General of Militia in Georgia and the Carolinas. In 1870 while in command of a battalion of his militia, they were surrounded by a superior force and he was killed in the battle. His untimely death brought to an end the production of this rifle for military use, but it continued to be made for sporting purposes notably by Durs Egg. All versions of the Ferguson rifle are rare and very much sought after.

The Baker rifle (plate 37), being the first British rifle to be

made on a reasonably large scale for issue to the army, makes it a good starting point for the average collector interested in military rifles. Ezekiel Baker's design for a rifle, accepted by the Board of Ordnance in 1800, may be said to be a military version of the German deer rifle. The heavy 30 inch barrel had seven groove rifling with a quarter turn in the barrel length. This rifle was designed to shoot a tightly patched ball and was accurate up to about 200 yards. The bayonet was distinctive, being sword hilted with a single edged blade 23 inches in length; this was however replaced from 1815 by a lighter socket bayonet or from 1823 by a light spike blade fixed to the original brass hilt.

The 95th or Rifle Regiment armed with the Baker rifle more than justified themselves in the Peninsular War. Their good but fluid discipline enabled them to seize an opportunity quickly to use their accurate fire to the greatest advantage. An incident at the siege of Babajoz in 1812 illustrates what a group of riflemen were able to achieve by accurate concentrated fire, by first diminishing, and finally silencing the fire of some heavy enemy cannon that were doing frightful execution to the British advanced artillery batteries. The 95th Rifles were re-styled the Rifle Brigade in 1816.

The riflemen in the Peninsula were proud of their skill and used to put it to good use during foraging expeditions by bagging for the pot such game as was available.

The Baker rifles did good service and were in production until 1838 when they were superceded by the Brunswick rifle. The Brunswick rifle was George Lovell's improved version of a rifle designed by Captain Berners, field adjutant to the Duke of Brunswick. The barrel was 30 inches in length with a calibre of ·704 and deep two groove rifling designed for firing a belted ball (the raised broad belt round the ball fitted the grooves of the rifling). The lock, used on the early models, was of the back

Plate 38
Rifleman of the 95th or Rifle Regiment with the Baker rifle, using the sling to assist taking a steady aim. Peninsular War period.

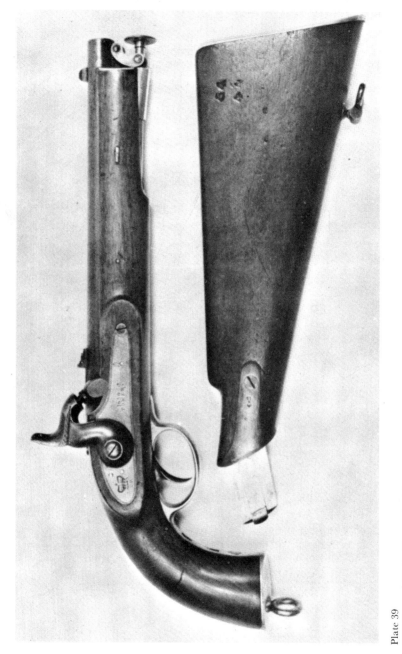

Plate 39

1856 Pattern rifled military pistol dated 1859 with Crown, VR and TOWER on lockplate. Detachable stock, swivel ramrod.

62

Plate 40
Adams' percussion revolver .50 calibre,
circa 1851.

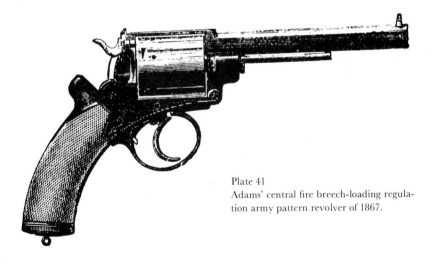

Plate 41
Adams' central fire breech-loading regulation army pattern revolver of 1867.

action type, that is the mainspring was behind the hammer. Percussion cap ignition was used for the new rifle, its adoption for military purposes being largely due to the persuasion of Lovell, who had been appointed to look into this question by the Board of Ordnance. After 1842 the normal forward action lock was used in place of Lovell's back action lock (plate 31 lower). Made in considerable numbers for the Army, Navy and East India Company, the Brunswick rifle had some advantage over the Baker so far as accurate range was concerned, but to offset this there were complaints about the difficulty of loading when the barrel became fouled after a few shots.

As a result of experiments in France with elongated expanding bullets, carried out by Captain Minié, the French and other nations, including Britain, adopted the principle. This type of bullet could be easily loaded but on being fired it expanded at the base to give a gas-tight fit and also key well into the rifling.

The Minié Rifled Musket of 1851 had a barrel of 39 inches in length and ·702 inches calibre, rifled with four grooves and firing a bullet with an iron cup-shaped wedge to assist its expansion. The powder charge was $2\frac{1}{2}$ drams. This was the first general issue rifle to the army as a whole, as opposed to those issued to rifle regiments only, and it filled the need moderately well until the first Enfield Rifle was adopted in 1853.

It was probably the Minié Rifled Musket in the hands of the men of the 93rd, the Sutherland Highlanders (formed 1799) that won them the only infantry battle honour at Balaclava 1854. They were the famous 'thin red line' that stood steady in the face of a furious charge by the Russian cavalry, halting and repulsing them by steady rifle fire.

The government run Enfield factory which had, since 1804, been mainly concerned with the assembling of the components of various arms, was in 1851 and 1852 expanded and equipped with the latest rifle making machinery from America. The 1853 Enfield rifle was then put into large scale production to meet the need for a better rifle for use in the Crimea. The original Enfield had a well proportioned overall shape and a 39 inch barrel of ·577 calibre rifled with three wide shallow grooves.

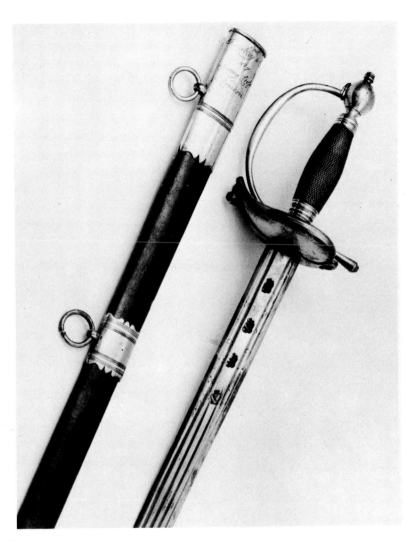

Plate 42

Heavy cavalry officer's dress sword pattern of 1796. Copper gilt hilt, grip bound with silver wire. Fitted with 17th century blade stamped with turbanned head marks and SAHAGUM. Scabbard of leather covered wood with three gilt mounts, the locket engraved 'Knubley & Co. No 7 Charing Cross London'.

The bullet was the hollow based Pritchett pattern to which was subsequently added a tapered boxwood plug to assist expansion. The rifle was also made in varying lengths and with minor changes in detail and later the rifling was changed to five grooves with a slightly increased twist. The bayonet was of the triangular socket type.

Though not entirely satisfactory the Enfield gave good service in the Crimea and Indian Mutiny and it was also bought in considerable numbers by Volunteers, during the French scare of 1859–62, who enthusiastically practised their marksmanship with it.

Enfield rifles have been popular in recent years with those collectors who enjoy putting their rifles to the test on the open range and several keen muzzle-loading rifle clubs have resulted.

Some criticism of the shooting of the Enfield rifle at longer

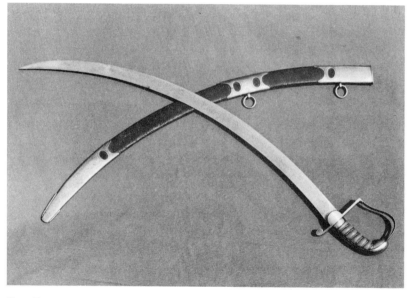

Plate 43
Stirrup hilted sabre of the type favoured by officers of the Rifle Regiment and Light Infantry. Early 19th century. Hilt and scabbard mounts of steel. Light flat sided blade.

ranges led to Sir Joseph Whitworth being asked to look into the question of rifling for small arms. Whitworth's solution was a hexagonal bore with slightly rounded corners of ·450 calibre and an elongated bullet cast from a hardened lead alloy which corresponded with the shape and twist of the rifling. At the trials held at Hythe in 1864 the Whitworth rifle shot with extraordinary accuracy and was superior at all ranges to the Enfield. At ranges between 1000 and 2000 yards, the difference was spectacular, for while the Whitworth remained accurate, the Enfield shot too wildly to be counted at 1400 yards.

This demonstration was conclusive as regards accuracy, but the Committee on Small Bore Rifles were quite right to reject Whitworth rifling for military weapons because of the great difficulty experienced in loading after a few shots, unless the bore was constantly wiped clean. Nevertheless the Whitworth rifle was very successful on the Wimbledon Rifle Range opened in 1860 by Queen Victoria, who pulled a silk cord to fire a fixed Whitworth rifle which threw its bullet within $1\frac{1}{2}$ inches of the centre of the target at 400 yards. It is not surprising that Whitworth rifles are keenly sought after by muzzle-loading enthusiasts, particularly if they are cased with their bullet moulds and other equipment.

Various rifles and carbines of an experimental nature were tried out by the Board of Ordnance and then a limited issue made to units of the army for further trial. Among these was the oval-bored rifle of Charles Lancaster issued in small numbers experimentally to the 1st Battalion of the Rifle Brigade during the Kaffir War, and later adopted as the arm of the Corps of Sappers and Miners in 1855.

Calisher and Terry's capping breech-loader was given an extensive trial on H.M.S. 'Excellent' in 1858 and issued experimentally to some cavalry units. The American Sharp's carbine was also bought and issued for a short period to cavalry.

Most notable of the capping breech-loading carbines was that produced by Westley Richards in 1858. It was named the 'monkey tail' because of the lever arm which lifted from the top of the grip to open the breech. This carbine had an octagonal version of the Whitworth type of rifling and was approved as the official cavalry arm in 1861 and was subsequently issued to Yeomanry Regiments.

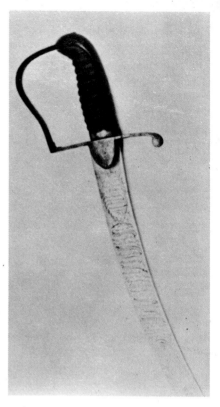

Plate 44
Stirrup hilted sabre with light curved flat sided blade engraved with the original owner's record of the battles and engagements as a British officer commanding the 11th Battalion of the Portuguese Cacadores (attached to the Rifle Regiment in the Peninsular War). Engraved between laurel leaves: 'Duke of Wellington Army, Sir Thos Picton Division, 11th Portuguese Cacadores'. Engravings on both sides of blade date from the 'Taking of Badajoz by storm 1812' to 'left arm being broke by a musket ball' in 1814. Presumably he then returned home and had his sword engraved.

The desirability of a breech-loading rifle for general issue, led to the adoption in 1865 of Jacob Snider's system for the conversion of the existing Enfield rifles to take a coiled paper cased, centre fire cartridge. The cartridge was improved and strengthened by Colonel Boxer in 1867. There followed the adoption in 1871 of the Martini-Henry rifle, with the Martini falling block action opened by a lever behind the trigger guard, and ·450 Henry rifling. This single shot rifle used a brass cased cartridge.

Colonel Colt's greatest success with the revolvers he showed at the Great Exhibition of 1851 was his sale of large numbers of his Navy pattern to the Board of Admiralty. Colt did not get all his own way however, for Robert Adams already had a five chamber, solid frame, self-cocking percussion revolver on show

at the 1851 Exhibition (plate 40). In 1853 the Rigby type of rammer was added, and the addition of Frederick Beaumont's double action, which enabled the hammer to be cocked by the thumb for accurate shooting or the trigger for quick shooting, made this Beaumont Adams revolver one of the best of its day. The qualities of the revolver did not escape the attention of the Board of Ordnance who, in 1856, officially adopted it in sizes of 38 and 54 bore. The percussion version being later followed by breech-loading models using metalic cartridges (plate 41).

Also worthy of note is the Webley revolver which commenced with the single action, long spur hammer model designed by James Webley. Various models were produced including a double action model taking the ·577 Boxer cartridge. The ·45 revolver, incorporating an automatic ejector, and manufactured to such precision that all the parts were interchangeable, was at last adopted in 1887 as the official revolver for the Army and Navy.

Looking back to the development of the military sword in the eighteenth century we find the modified versions of the cavalry basket hilted broadsword being replaced about 1760 by a single edged grooved blade with a hilt having a ring guard, knuckle bow with one or two additional bars, and the pommel large and rounded. The fashion for regiments of light cavalry in the style of the Hungarian Hussars, which spread throughout most of Europe, led to the adoption about 1780 of a curved cavalry sabre for units of British light cavalry. The first British light cavalry to be officially named Hussars were the 7th, 10th, and 15th Light Dragoons in 1805. Lancers in the style of the Polish Lancers were introduced from 1815.

In 1796 the regulation heavy cavalry trooper's sword was a great meat chopper of a sword with a straight, broad 32 inch blade with deep fullers (wide shallow grooves) and a 'hatchet' or curved point. The hilt had a pierced iron disc guard. About the same date a beautifully balanced steel stirrup hilted sabre was adopted for light cavalry. This sabre had a broad fullered blade slightly broader towards the curved point. This sword proved to be murderously effective as a cutting weapon in action.

Through the eighteenth century officers' swords show considerable variation, being privately made for them by the various sword cutlers, having copper gilt hilts and etched, blued and gilt blades. The typical officer's sword of the second half of the eighteenth century has a heart shaped guard, knuckle bow and oval pommel but by the end of the century the infantry officer's sword will usually have a light butterfly shaped guard which hinges down on the near side for ease of wearing. Light cavalry and light infantry mostly favoured stirrup hilted sabres (plate 43) while heavy cavalry officers had long straight single-edged grooved bladed swords with pierced copper gilt hilts bearing their regimental crest. Many officers during the Napoleonic War while having their dress swords made more or less to regulation pattern, often used any sword they happened to fancy for active service, in the same way that they used privately made pistols. The handy little sabre engraved with its 'battle honours' carried in the Peninsular campaign by an infantry officer is a good example (plate 44).

Volunteer officers' swords were very much left to the choice or lattitude of their colonels. The example shown which was made for an officer of the Loyal St James's Volunteers is typical of a popular style for infantry officers (plate 45).

Early in the nineteenth century there was a considerable fashion among officers for the Mameluke or Turkish style of sabre, recognised in the form of the official General Officer's sabre of 1831, which has remained the regulation pattern since.

Much of the pleasure to be derived in forming a collection of swords of this period is to be found in the interesting variations and the superb work of the sword cutlers, at a time when the sword was still very much a fighting weapon.

Turning to Naval weapons, perhaps the most fruitful and exciting period is the era of fighting sail associated with Britain's greatest Admiral, Horatio Nelson. It is also fitting to recall that many of Nelson's early triumphs, that were to mark him out as a man of exceptional leadership, were led by him sword in hand. His first success, when Post Captain of the Frigate Hinchingbroke, was the leading of the assault and capture of the inland fort of San Juan during attacks made on the Spanish in the Caribbean in 1780.

When in command of the Agamemnon he took part in many land actions leading to the conquest of Corsica during 1793 and 1794, losing an eye during the attack on Calvi.

In the encounter with the Spanish fleet off Cape St Vincent, while serving under the flag of Admiral Sir John Jervis, Commodore Nelson on his own initiative ordered his ship to leave the line of battle to prevent the escape of the Spanish ships. His ship 'Captain' being partially disabled by enemy gunfire, he ordered it to close with the nearest Spanish ship, the San Joseph. It was hardly the thing for a Commodore to do, but charactersistically Nelson led the boarding party in person, and when another Spanish ship, the San Nicolas, came alongside to help the San Joseph, Nelson ordered a further boarding party to attack across the decks of the San Joseph. After a brisk

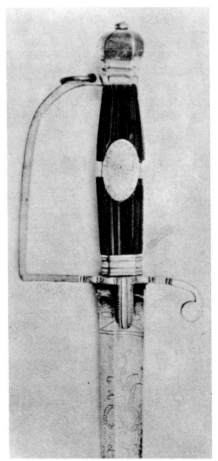

Plate 45
Officer's Spadroon of the Loyal St James's Volunteers (raised 1797). Gilt hilt with fluted ebony grip. Straight 32 inch blade etched with Royal arms and military trophies.

71

fight Nelson received the swords of the defeated Spaniards on the quarter deck, taking both ships as prizes. Nelson was later to lose his arm leading the attack on Tenerife and to fight and win the major battles of his career: the Nile 1798, Copenhagen 1801 and his final blaze of glory, the great victory of Trafalgar 1805.

The weapons used by sailors and marines fighting on deck, in boarding parties, or in land assaults, were: boarding pikes, cutlasses, pistols, muskets and bayonets. The officers were armed with swords and pistols.

There were patterns of pistol and musket specifically designed for sea service, but in times of shortage the numbers were often made up from oddments of arms no longer required by the army. Sea service pistols often have belt hooks and some were issued without provision for a ramrod. Sea service muskets were generally shorter, for convenience of use in cramped fighting conditions.

The regulation officer's dress sword of the Napoleonic War period was of the straight fullered single-edge type, with a copper gilt stirrup hilt. The langets, small U-shaped extensions from the hilt over the blade, had engraved upon them the Naval foul anchor (plate 46 left). Later patterns have the lion's head pommel combined with the backstrap which remained a standard feature of naval swords (plate 46 centre), and to which was added in 1827 the gilt half basket guard with the crowned anchor badge on the outside (plate 46 right).

There was during the Napoleonic War, a fairly loose interpretation of the regulation dress patterns, but so far as fighting swords were concerned, the officers chose any handy sort of sword they fancied. Midshipmen seem to have gone in for various sorts of fanciful dirks from time to time, but the straight-bladed type with a copper gilt and ivory hilt, with quillons turned down or with one up and one down, seems to have been most popular during the Napoleonic War period (colour plate 10).

Of particular interest amongst naval weapons is the seven barrelled volley gun designed by Henry Nock. Some of these had smooth and others rifled barrels which fired together giving a good chance of at least one of the seven balls cutting an enemy sniper from the rigging.

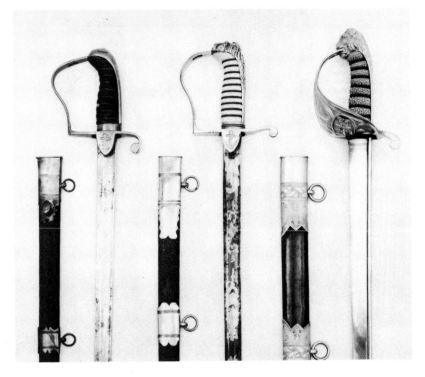

Plate 46

Left. Naval Officer's regulation pattern sword of 1805-1827 for Lieutenants and Midshipmen. Gilt stirrup hilt with shagreen grip and foul anchors engraved on the langets. Straight 32 inch blade etched with Royal cypher and Naval trophies. Scabbard leather with gilt mounts.

Centre. Naval Officer's regulation pattern sword of 1805-1827 for Commanders and above. Gilt stirrup hilt with lion's head pommel, langets engraved with foul anchors and the grip of ivory. Straight 32 inch blade gilt and blued. Scabbard leather with gilt mounts. Inscription on locket records that the sword was presented to Commander Edward Carry-Astley in 1819.

Right. Naval Officer's sword 1827 pattern. Gilt Gothic half basket hilt with lion's head pommel and crowned anchor on guard. Slightly curved quill-back blade etched with the Royal arms, anchor and Prosser maker to the King London. Has elaborate scabbard introduced . in 1832 for Flag Officers. Formally the property of Admiral Sir James de Saumarez G C B (1757–1836) who was second in command to Nelson at the Battle of the Nile.

73

74

Most desirable are the presentation swords awarded from the Lloyd's patriotic fund to Naval Officers who distinguished themselves in action. The gilt and decorated hilt and scabbards are a fitting setting for the richly blued and gilt blade on which is told the story of the heroic action for which the award was made. These swords were made in various grades according to rank, from £30 swords for Mates and Midshipmen, to £100 swords for Captains and Commanders (plate 47).

Plate 47
Lloyd's Patriotic Fund Sword of the fifty pound type. Hilt with ormolu mounts and ivory grip. Blade blued and inscribed in gilt 'From the Patriotic Fund at Lloyds to Lieut. Thos. Robt. Pye of the Royal Marines of H.M.S. Boadecea severely wounded in a gallant attack on the Enemy at St Paul in the Isle of Bourbon on 21st September 1809.'

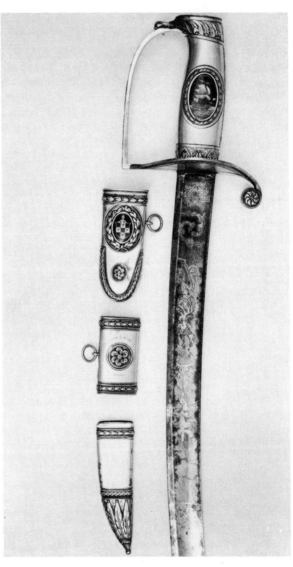

Plate 48
Fine English presentation sabre. Silver
gilt, set with enamel plaques. Presented by
The Committee of Merchants of London
to Lieutenant John Buller in 1797. Maker
John Morrisset.

3. Sporting weapons

Hunting was for many centuries the favourite pastime of noblemen throughout Europe and in the course of time specific hunting weapons were developed and suitably enriched.

For the hunting of the stag and wild boar with hounds, a hunting sword developed similar to the short self-protection sword known as the hanger. The hunting sword of the eighteenth century (plate 49) usually has a blade not much more than two feet in length, some two-edged, and some curved but most are of the straight single-edged type. The hilts are of great interest for their variety of design, workmanship and the materials used, such as horn, ivory, agate and stag's horn. The quillons are often finished with animal heads and sometimes there is a knuckle bow or chain. Typical of many is the 'shell' that overhangs the top of the blade, usually enriched with a hunting scene cast and chased in high relief.

Because of the savage nature of the wild boar when brought to bay, powerful spears were used to settle with him. These boar spears have broad leaf-shaped blades and a cross bar. An interesting nineteenth-century boar spear combined the spear point with a short percussion cap barrel; the lock being

77

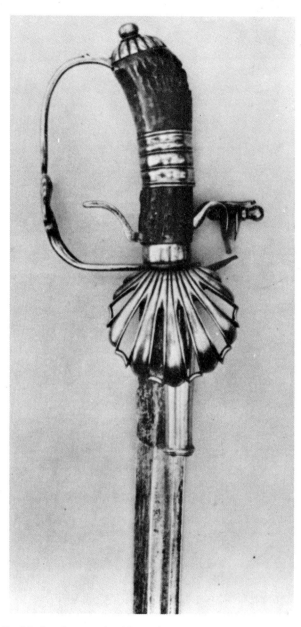

Plate 49 English hunting sword with steel mounts
and stagshorn grip combined with a pistol. *Circa* 1740.

78

triggered off by the thrust of the spear.

In France and particularly in Germany where the chase was attended with considerable ceremonial, very fine Waldpraxe or Trousse de chasse were made, consisting of a broad, heavy chopping knife in its sheath attended by a number of smaller knives and instruments. Often richly decorated with animals of the chase, they were used for cutting up deer or removing heads for trophies from such animals as the wild boar.

In parts of Europe, crossbows of various kinds for shooting bolts at deer or stones at birds, were gradually superseded by matchbox guns and rifles in the sixteenth century. Because it was necessary to keep a slow-match cord smouldering and move it forward in the serpentine as it burned back, these matchlock guns were awkward to manage in the circumstances that arise when stalking wild beasts. However in the first quarter of the sixteenth century two inventions greatly improved the gun as a hunting weapon. The wheel-lock gave it a form of ignition that could be kept ready for instant use for any length of time, and the rifling of the barrel increased the accurate range.

While the nobility used fine wheel-lock guns for hunting, the peasantry were not slow to appreciate the advantage of match-lock guns of the simplest sort as a means of filling the pot in winter. This could not be described as sporting shooting, for it was a matter of necessity to get as close as possible to sitting birds before firing a charge of small shot at them.

The simple peasant guns have disappeared but fine quality sixteenth century matchlock and wheel-lock guns survived in the noble armouries of Europe, mainly because of their value as works of art with their chiselled and engraved metalwork and elaborate bone or stag's horn inlay. The best guns of this period rarely come onto the market and when they do they fetch very high prices.

The seventeenth century saw the development of the flint-lock ignition. The earliest examples of the snaphaunce lock belong to the sixteenth century, their use becoming general in the seventeenth century. However, first in the English lock and then in the French lock, the steel and pan cover were combined in the simple and practical flintlock that lasted with minor improvements until the first quarter of the nineteenth century.

With the flintlock was developed a lighter type of fowling

piece with a shoulder stock that was practical for use in the increasingly popular art of shooting birds flying. This sport of shooting flying birds had already been widely adopted by the nobility of Europe, when in 1660 King Charles II was restored to the throne of England. He and his courtiers brought back with them French fowling pieces and a taste for this new sport.

Many of the seventeenth century fowling pieces that remain are of very fine quality, gracefully enriched with chiselled and engraved metalwork and stocked in exotically grained woods. Long single-barrelled guns are typical but a few double-barrelled guns were made of the over and under, swivel beech type. A single cock was then able to serve both frizzens when the under barrel was turned to the top.

The characteristic of seventeenth and early eighteenth century fowling pieces is the length of the barrels, these being between three and four feet, their lengths being made necessary by the comparatively slow rate of burning of the gunpowder. The eighteenth century saw the fowling piece refined into a graceful well-balanced gun which was as great a delight to handle as it was pleasing to look upon.

A notable factor in the improvement of the eighteenth century gun, was the use throughout much of Europe, of the strong and resilient Spanish barrels (plate 50). These barrels were so much admired that the general style of them was copied, and in some cases they were deliberately forged. The typical Spanish barrel is octagonal for the first third and round for the remainder, the join being set off by a band of chiselled decoration. The name of the barrel maker, his mark and town are usually impressed on gold on the top flat of the barrel and sometimes set off with decorative gold inlay work. The high quality of these Spanish barrels was due to the very fine iron

Plate 50
Fine Spanish flintlock gun signed on the barrel 'EN MADRID JOACHIN DE ZELAIA ANNO DE 1758'. The maker's stamp in gold on the barrel and lock. Barrel richly inlaid with gold and lock chiseled with figure of Diana and hound against a gold ground. Note that the French style of lock has been used.

80

81

Plate 51
Detail of silver wire inlay on an English
fowling piece by Delany, London, *circa*
1725.

from which they were made, and the method by which they
were forged ensuring that the grain of the iron went round the
barrel instead of along it.

Eighteenth century fowling pieces are reasonably available,
although competition is keen for the finest examples, Silver
mounts were much favoured for good quality guns, the heel-
plate, trigger guard, side plate and escutcheon for instance were
engraved and chiselled with elegant designs. In addition the
stocks were inlaid with silver wire in delicate foliated curves
and tendrils (plate 51). On the continent, the stocks were, to a
greater or lesser extent carved, but the English guns rarely have
more than perhaps a formalised shell design behind the barrel
tang.

A useful pointer to the date of English eighteenth century
guns is given by the design in front of the trigger guard. In the
first half of the century this part was finished in varying forms
of a trefoil design, about 1750 this changed to an acorn, and
towards the end of the century it was replaced by the pineapple
design that remained popular until the middle of the nineteenth century. Although more double-barrelled sporting guns
were made on the continent in the second half of the eighteenth

century they were still the exception rather than the rule. This was particularly so in Britain where double-barrelled guns did not begin to overtake the numbers of single until the first quarter of the nineteenth century.

The combination of the manufacture of better quality gunpowder with the new patent breech designed by the great gunmaker Henry Nock in 1787, made 30 inch barrels a practical proposition. The effect of the patent breech was to make more speedy and consistent the burning of the powder charge by causing the first ignition to blast a flame through the whole charge. The 30 inch barrel enabled double guns to be built which were of reasonable weight and good balance. Another factor which enabled barrels to be made lighter, stronger and more resilient was the method of forging barrels from ribbons of high quality iron. These ribbons of iron were wound in a spiral round and along a hardened steel mandril so that the edges were in contact. The twisted spiral was then heated to white heat, 'jumped' on the mandril to bring the edges tight together and then welded by hammer blows on a U-shaped anvil with the mandril inside the coil. After being thoroughly welded, the barrel was well hammered when cold to condense and toughen the metal. The barrel was bored until all the scale was removed on the inside and then ground to the right shape and thickness from the outside. Because the grain of the metal went round the barrel it was better able to stand the lateral stress. The lighter barrels that resulted meant that a double gun with good handling qualities was a practical proposition. Incidentally the barrels were known as stub twist barrels because of the stubs or old horse shoe nails from which they were forged.

In the second half of the eighteenth century the flintlock was improved by the addition of a small wheel bearing between the frizzen and its spring, and inside the lock the friction between the tumbler and mainspring was eliminated by a steel swivel. The metal round the pan was also partially cut away to assist in draining rain away from the pan. The latter part of the eighteenth century saw the rise of some of the greatest English gunmakers like Joseph Griffin who in the 1770s joined Tow to become Griffin and Tow, John Twigg and his foreman John Manton who set up on his own in 1782, and his brother Joseph

83

who left him to start his business in 1789. The plain but very finely finished style of guns for which John Twigg was noted was continued by John and Joe Manton. Silver furniture was replaced by iron, silver wire inlay disguarded and the fore part of the half stock held by a single bolt or side nail fastening. These guns however achieve a graceful elegance to which the beauty of their brown twist barrels and their walnut stocks add character, while the only ornament is the unobtrusive engraving of the lock and furniture.

The Manton brothers particularly Joe Manton brought the flintlock double gun to perfection. The strongly sprung cock was made to fire with a short action, the pan of a V (colour plate 11) or narrow U-shape was rendered more rainproof by cutting away additional metal round it. The breech too was cut away to bring the touch-hole nearer the centre of the breech; this helped to speed up ignition and also enabled the two locks to be set in closer, making the gun neater.

Apart from speeding up ignition Joe Manton's patent elevated rib caused the gun to throw the shot high of the point of aim enabling the shooter to keep his target in view. Also as many of the shots taken were at rising birds, walked up with dogs, it was a help to those who failed to give sufficient allowance above the bird.

All the fine flintlock sporting guns of the late eighteenth and first quarter of the nineteenth century are particularly desirable as collectors' pieces so it is not surprising that good examples are now increasingly scarce. Though good guns were also made by a variety of makers, the name of Manton (plate 54) and especially Joe Manton, carries extra weight not least because of Joe's association with the famous Colonel Peter Hawker who immortalised him and his guns in his book 'Instructions to Young Sportsmen in all that relates to Guns and Shooting' first published in 1814. Colonel Hawker's views on guns and shooting, put down in his characteristically direct manner, were the result of untiring trial and experiment in the field. He was an enthusiastic wildfowler with punt gun and shoulder gun along the salt marshes, at a time when such shooting was mostly left to professionals and locals shooting for the pot. Joseph Manton made two of Peter Hawker's favourite guns, fondly named 'Old Joe' which was his nineteen bore double-

Colour plate 13
Rifle, J. Lang.

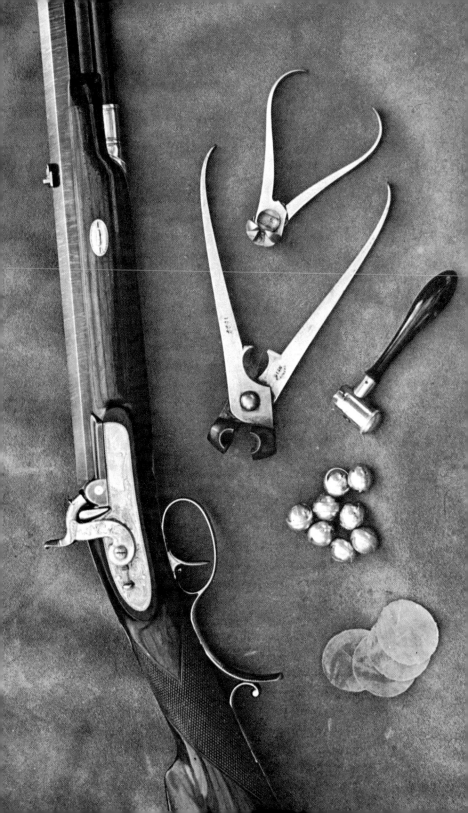

game gun, and 'Big Joe' his single-barrel five bore duck gun weighing 19 pounds.

Hawker also had a high opinion of the guns made by Westley Richards of Birmingham many of which were sold through the London agency of William Bishop, a celebrated London character who was known as 'The Bishop of Bond Street'.

Useful as a guide to the date of the early nineteenth century guns is the change from the use of gold for touch holes, to platinum, between 1805 and 1810.

At a time when the flintlock was reaching its last stages of development there came the first experiments with the use of detonating powder which were soon to challenge and eventually end the long reign of flint and steel. Alexander John Forsyth, minister of Belhelvie in Scotland, first patented a system for the use of detonating powder in 1807. The early system involving a magazine and loose powder was rather too complicated for widespread application. Gunmakers tried out many ways of containing the powder in pills, discs, tubes, tapes and caps. However it was eventually the copper cap with powder in the top that was to prove most widely acceptable,

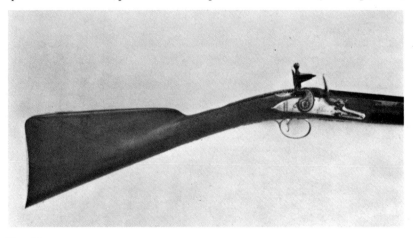

Plate 52
Light 28 bore fowling piece by Sikes of Sheffield *circa* 1775. Silver wire decoration behind the breech. Typical 18th century stock with slender grip and considerable bend.

Colour plate 14
Old Shekarry and bear.

and was to make even the quickest flintlock seem slow by comparison. Any rare or unusual forms of early percussion ignition are well worth collecting.

The quickness, reliability and simplicity of the percussion cap gave a fresh impetus to gunmaking and sporting shooting. From the early 1820s until about 1860 they were made in large numbers in many qualities from a Joe Manton at 60 guineas to Birmingham double guns produced for as little as £2 with skelp twist barrels or £1 for one with barrels of 'Sham damn iron' which rather speaks for itself. Fine percussion guns are of course most desirable collectors' items especially if they genuinely bear the names of the best makers, and if the guns are in good order, the pleasure of shooting with them can be added to that of possessing them. Obviously, as the prices quoted indicate, there is a very great difference between the quality of the best and the cheapest percussion shot guns. The quality of a gun can be judged by its balance, graceful lines and the perfection of fit and finish of all its parts. The quantity of engraving is no guide, but restrained engraving of the finest quality usually indicates a good gun.

It was increasingly the custom in the nineteenth century to case the better quality guns in fine mahogany cases lined with baize, with compartments for all that was necessary for loading and cleaning. These cases usually have on the inside of the lids the trade label of the gunmaker, often an elaborate example of copper plate engraving. Cases complete with all their fittings and a clean trade label, very much enhance the desirability of a good gun and of course its value.

When Joseph Manton went bankrupt in 1826, the position he had held was taken by two of the great men in English gunmaking, James Purdey (plate 56) and Charles Lancaster. James Purdey had worked for Joe Manton and, after leaving to work as manager for Forsyth, he started on his own in 1814, taking over Joe Manton's Oxford Street premises in 1826. Charles Lancaster had for many years supplied his finely bored

Plate 53
Engraving from The Shooting Directory by Thornhill, 1804, showing sportsman priming the pan of his fowling piece.

87

Plate 54
Double barrelled flintlock gun by John Manton *circa* 1800. Spur cocks and rain proof pans. Stub twist barrels.

Plate 55
Engraving of pheasant shooting from The Shooting Directory by Thornhill, 1804. Walking up the birds with the aid of pointers.

barrels to the Mantons, but in 1826 he set up as a gunmaker, soon gaining the highest reputation for his guns.

Apart from percussion game guns of between sixteen and twelve bore, there were considerable numbers of long barrelled duck guns of from eight to four bore. These duck guns should not be confused with the big bore guns made for the popular sport of shooting pigeons released from traps. These single barrel pigeon guns can usually be distinguished from wildfowl guns by their shorter barrels, fine finish and because many of them lack provision for a ramrod; a loading rod being supplied in the case. Double-barrelled pigeon guns of twelve bore gauge firing $1\frac{1}{4}$ ounces of shot later became standard; percussion guns of this type, without provision for a ramrod, were still being made in the late 1860s.

Trap pigeon shooting had started in the early nineteenth century in a free and easy style, often by a convenient public house. The 'Old Hats' public house at Eaiing got its name from its early association with pigeon shooting, the old hats being

Plate 56
Double barrelled percussion sporting gun
by James Purdey 1837

90

placed over small holes in the ground to serve as makeshift traps; the pigeon being released by a long cord attached to the hat. The 'sport' soon became highly competitive with rich prizes and much gambling. This in turn led to the growth of 'professionals' using guns of large bore to gain advantage. However the rules were later tightened to curb the unscrupulous, and properly organised meetings took place at bona fide clubs like the Red House Club, Battersea, Hornsey Wood House and later the Hurlingham and the Gun Club, Notting Hill. These gun clubs fulfilled much the same function for guns as motor racing now does for cars: all the leading gunmakers being constantly in attendance, for reputations and sales were to be gained by the makers of the guns used by successful shooters. The sport flourishes today with the use now of the inanimate 'bird' or clay pigeon.

The pinfire breech-loading gun with drop-down barrels, by the Frenchman Lefaucheux, was exhibited at the Great Exhibition of 1851. It proved to be the starting point from which the modern game gun was eventually to be developed. Joseph Lang was the first English gunmaker to bring out his version soon after the exhibition, and numerous others followed with their particular methods of ensuring a stronger closure of the breech (plate 57). Many of these early breech-loaders are reasonably available at moderate prices, but are likely to appreciate in value as interest in them grows. Apart from a variety of pinfire guns there are also remarkable guns like Charles Lancaster's centre fire gun and cartridge of 1852 which was well in advance of its time, and the needlefire gun introduced by William Needham in 1850.

The introduction in 1861 by George Daw of the centre fire cartridge, virtually the modern game cartridge, gave fresh impetus to the breech-loader, leading first to the production of fine hammer guns (plate 58) and then to hammerless and ejector guns before the end of the century. Particularly worthy of note were: the Purdey bolt, an efficient snap action closure operated by the familiar top lever, the marvellously simple Anson and Deeley hammerless action of 1875, the father of almost all modern box-lock actions, and then there followed the graceful and ingenious self-opening sidelock action designed by Frederick Beesley for James Purdey in 1880.

91

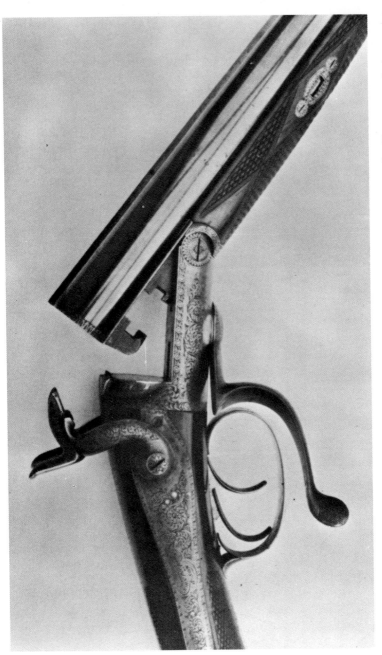

Plate 57 Double barrelled 12 bore pinfire gun by John Dickson of Edinburgh, 1863. Back action locks, large overhead hammers, under lever, screw action. Damascus barrels.

Guns of this period have the added interest and attraction of fine Damascus barrels forged in a variety of styles from twisted rods of alternate iron and steel; the pattern being shown by the light colour of the steel against the darker iron, brought out by the process of browning. Steel barrels began to replace Damascus from the 1880s.

All the good quality early centre-fire hammer and hammerless guns are likely to increase in value as interest is growing rapidly in this great period of English gunmaking, remarkable for superb craftsmanship combined with an extraordinary fertility of invention.

Returning to the sporting rifle, we find the Germans greatly attached to their wheel-lock rifles which were still being made in the early years of the eighteenth century. In Silesia an

Plate 58
Double barrelled 12 bore centre fire gun by Pape of Newcastle *circa* 1868. Early snap action with thumb lever to right front of trigger guard, rebounding locks, Damascus barrels.

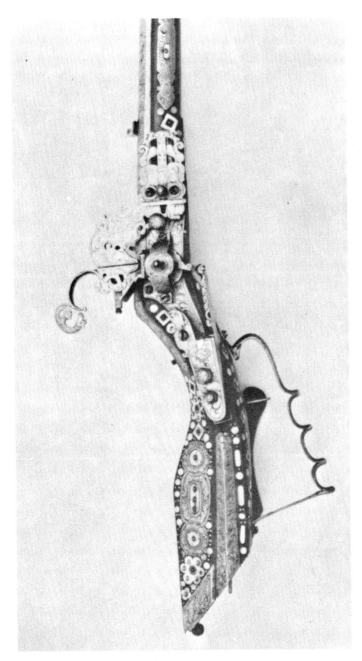

Plate 59
Silesian Tschinke, 17th century. A light birding rifle, the wheel-lock having an external mainspring.

94

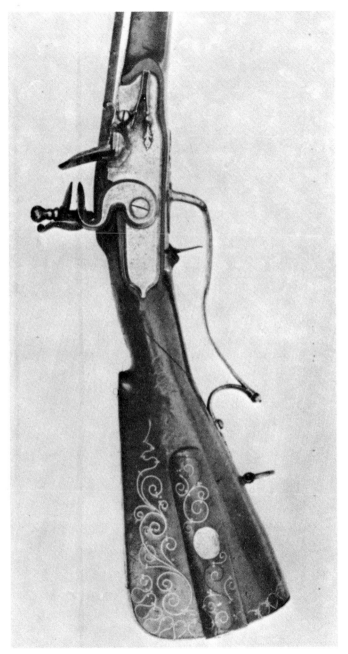

Plate 60
German flintlock Jäger or sporting rifle *circa* 1700 with steel wire inlay on butt and sliding wooden patch box. Heavy octagonal barrel.

interesting light birding rifle (plate 59) was developed, having a wheel-lock with an external mainspring, a stock designed to be rested against the cheek, elaborately enriched with engraved brass and inlay work. These rifles were used for shooting such birds as pheasants when they had been flushed up into trees by dogs. The rifle that was to have a widespread influence on rifle design in Europe in the eighteenth century was the German Jäger or hunter's rifle which at last superceded the wheel-lock. This Jäger rifle (plate 60) had a large calibre octagonal barrel with multigroove rifling, designed for a tightly patched ball that had to be rammed with considerable force or even hammered down. The stock was of the shoulder type with a cheekpiece and a sliding patch box on the other side. The wheel-lock was at last replaced by a flintlock of the French type and a set trigger was fitted. This type of rifle soon became the standard rifle for use against such animals as the deer, boar, bear and wolf.

In Britain there was, until the nineteenth century, a very limited need for rifles: these were mainly used for shooting deer kept in large parks, so eighteenth and early nineteenth century flintlock rifles are rare. However the enjoyment of the Scottish Highlands by Queen Victoria and Prince Albert and his love of deer stalking did much to make this sport popular. The railway helped by making the Highlands more easily accessible.

Plate 61
Typical English single barrel percussion sporting rifle *circa* 1830 by Nock, London. Heavy octagonal twist barrel with multigroove rifling.

Plate 62
Typical English percussion double barrelled rifle by James Purdey, 1844. Stock
with circular iron patch box and cheek
piece on the other side. 16 bore multigroove rifled barrels.

In addition to the increased demand for deer stalking rifles,
there was a demand for rifles for use in the vast hunting grounds
of Asia and Africa by officers, officials, explorers and hunters
who acquired a taste for the hitherto undreamed of opportunities for big game shooting.

The typical nineteenth century flint, and later percussion cap
rifle followed much the same general pattern as the German
hunting rifle, except for the plainer finish of the English version
(plate 61) and the substitution, from about 1830, of a round
iron patch box in the butt instead of the sliding German type.

The deer rifle of sixteen to twenty bore was no match for the
large and dangerous animals of Africa and India as many
hunters discovered the hard way. Doctor Livingstone was
badly mauled by a lion having wounded it with a rifle designed
for deer: he was attacked while in the act of reloading. This
incident illustrates the two main problems facing the hunter:
the need for a very powerful rifle and also a second shot in
reserve. The normal patched ball had to be shot with a moder-

ate powder charge, because too great a charge caused it to strip across the rifling, losing its accuracy. Faced with this problem some hunters preferred smooth bore ball guns designed to take very powerful charges, but accurate only to about 50 yards. The compromise solution was that of deep two groove rifling designed for a belted ball or conical bullet cast with raised 'wings' which fitted into the two groove rifling. These rifles could stand very large powder charges without stripping, and were reasonably accurate. The great hunter and explorer, Sir Samuel Baker, had one of the first of this type made to his specification by George Gibbs of Bristol. This prodigious rifle weighed 22 pounds, fired a 3 oz belted ball or 4 oz conical bullet, propelled by 16 drams of powder. When this load is compared with the 1 oz ball propelled by only $1\frac{1}{2}$ drams of powder of the typical deer rifle, its tremendous power can be imagined; Baker was to owe his life on more than one occasion to its ability to deliver a crushing knock-down blow to charging elephant or buffalo.

The need for a quick second shot was often vital when dealing with dangerous animals, in circumstances where reliance on a second gun being handed forward by a bearer was rather chancey.

Double barrelled rifles became increasingly popular from the 1830s onward (plate 62), multigroove rifling being generally superceded by the two groove type in the 1840s, and 1850s. To sight in a single barrel is relatively easy, but to solder two barrels together so that they converge together at the right angle to enable the sights along the centre rib to serve both barrels equally, certainly tests the art of the rifle maker to the full.

Double rifles have round barrels and broad flat ribs in which the sights are set. Best quality rifles were sold in finely fitted cases containing all that might be needed for loading, cleaning and maintenance in remote places (plate 63). In this condition

Plate 63
Fine quality two-groove sporting rifle by Joseph Lang, London, 1853. Cased with all original fittings needed for loading and cleaning.

98

Plate 64

A tricky situation when elephant hunting in the days of the muzzle-loader. The hunter having fired, finds his horse too scared to be remounted as two elephants charge. He was saved only by the persistence of his dogs that managed to draw off the elephants and give him a chance to remount.

Colour plate 15
Kentucky rifle.

100

they are particularly desirable especially if a collector also wishes to test their shooting capabilities, for without the original bullet mould and information about the intended load it is difficult to give them a fair trial. This is particularly so with a two groove rifle which lacks its mould, for a suitable belted ball or conical bullet mould will be very hard to find. Some of the fitted cases even have spare main and sear springs for the locks and a variety of tools, the use for some of which can be quite a puzzle.

There is a tendency to call almost any rifle of about sixteen bore upwards an elephant or big game rifle but the gun most popular for shooting elephant for ivory in Southern Africa was in fact a plain four bore duck gun. These guns, usually of the commonest sort made in Birmingham, had barrels shortened to about 30 inches, and are sometimes strengthened by shrinking rawhide to bind together lock, stock and barrel. This rawhide is said to be taken from the inside of the elephant's ear. These rough and ready guns loaded with a handful of coarse powder and a quarter pound ball, shot with tremendous power and were accurate enough for the close ranges at which most elephants were shot. A few of these guns were rifled but most were smooth and could be bought for about £6 in Africa: the famous hunter, Frederick Courtney Selous, shot his first seventy elephants with this sort of gun in the early 1870s.

Some hunters relied on riding down their quarry, shooting from the saddle or dismounted to shoot on foot when their quarry had been brought to bay by dogs (plate 64). However, for hunting on the open Veldt, a rifle that became known as a Cape rifle gained popularity; this expression was used for a double long barrelled two groove rifle with a broad flat rib.

Colour plate 16
Navy pattern colt.

The expression was also used for a gun with one barrel rifled and the other smooth. Though generally breech-loading on the systems used for shotguns, was applied later to rifles, there were a few pinfire rifles made in the 1850s and early 1860s. It was not until brass cased centre fire cartridges were combined with strong, reliable actions in the 1870s that breech-loading rifles really took over from muzzle-loaders.

Muzzle and early breech-loading rifles (plate 65) recall an age of robust sport, adventure and exploration in many lands, where hunters found it necessary to brave hardships, danger and sickness as well as many months of hard travel in remote country. Amongst the hunters and explorers were some who have vividly recorded their adventures, so we can, through their books, relive with them the wild free life, and turn to look with renewed interest at the rifles associated with the era of the Mighty Nimrods.

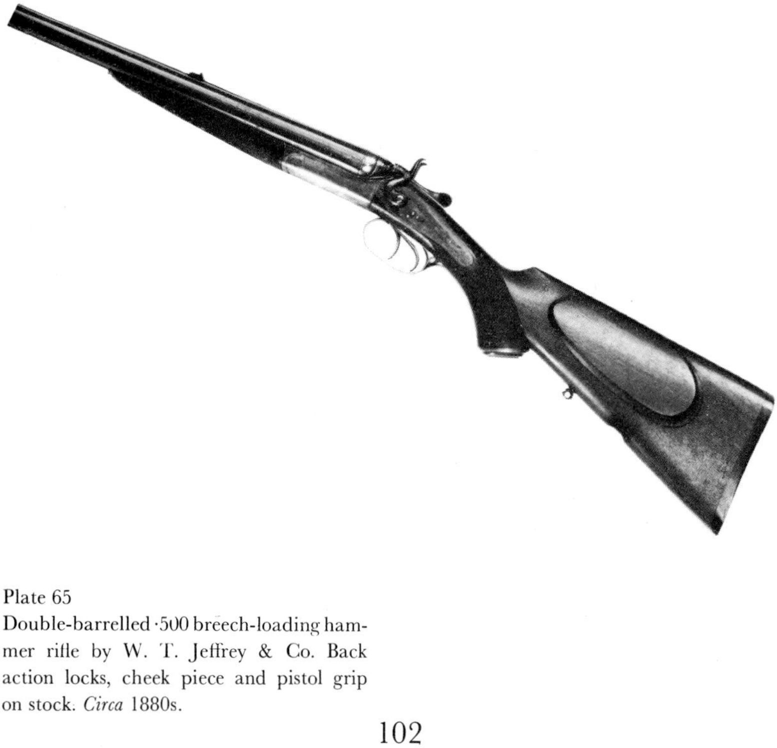

Plate 65
Double-barrelled ·500 breech-loading hammer rifle by W. T. Jeffrey & Co. Back action locks, cheek piece and pistol grip on stock. *Circa* 1880s.

4. Weapons of the American frontier

Vast numbers of books and films have been written on the saga of the American West, of the frontiersmen, Indians, U.S. cavalry, cowpunchers, outlaws and lawmen. It is hardly surprising that in America and many other parts of the world, there is widespread interest in the weapons associated with the old West.

In the seventeenth century smooth bore muskets had been used to protect the pioneer settlements from marauding Indians, but the eighteenth century was to see the development of a distinctive type of rifle, suited to the need of the frontiersmen, the use of which became general around the middle of the century.

Amongst the settlers arriving in America in the early eighteenth century, were gunsmiths of German, Swiss and French Huguenot origin, who settled in Pennsylvania. At first they made rifles of the German hunting type generally known as Jäger rifles, with their heavy hexagonal large bore barrels designed for a tightly fitting patched ball, that needed to be hammered down.

After a period of transition the typical American frontier

rifle emerged about the time of the War of Independence, 1775–1783. This rifle had a longer octagonal barrel of from about 42 to 46 inches with a smaller bore, from about ·50 of an inch calibre or thirty seven balls to the pound, to ·60 of an inch or twenty one balls to the pound. They were full stocked, that is up to the muzzle, in ripple grained maple, giving a tiger stripe effect. The angle of the butt has a pronounced bend and a deeply concave heel plate. Other characteristic features are the cheek piece embellished with scroll carving, the large hinged

Plate 66
Kentucky flintlock rifle by Jacob Kunts of Philadelphia, Pennsylvania (1770–1817). Rare double barrelled turnover type, barrels released to turn by pulling back the trigger guard. Fine engraved patch box and other brass inlay in ripple grained maple stock.

patch box with its scroll edged brass surround neatly inlaid into the butt, and sometimes simple symbolic designs such as an eight-pointed star were inlaid. The locks were mostly imported from England or Germany (plate 66).

The overall shape of these rifles is graceful, but they were also most practical for the frontiersmen. The smaller ball enabled more to be carried, and the longer barrel made the use of a more loosely patched ball that could be easily loaded, a practical possibility. The slower burning colonial quality powder was ideal for these rifles, giving the progressive pro-pulsion for which the long barrels were suited, thereby ensuring the maximum velocity without the ball stripping across the rifling.

The percussion 'Kentucky' rifles of the nineteenth century generally have barrels of reduced length and bore, and are of lighter weight. They also have a greater amount of decorative inlay of brass or silver, with more elaborate engraving on the patch box itself. The rifle was ideal both for hunting and for use

Plate 67
Colt 'Texas' Paterson holster pistol of ·36 calibre with 9 inch rifled barrel. *Circa* 1840. This pistol has the unusual feature of a folding trigger which lowers when the hammer is cocked.

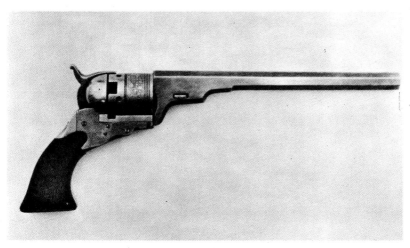

against marauding Indians. These elegant and accurate rifles are of course most desirable, for their place in the development of the rifle, and for their historic associations with frontier heroes like Daniel Boone and the fights between pioneers and Indians. Complementary to the Kentucky rifles are the cow horn powder flasks that are particularly attractive when engraved with designs which include maps showing forts and battles, ships and a variety of naive scenes (colour plate 15).

The constant demand for more arms both for wars and self-protection brought about a revolution in gunmaking. The name of Samuel Colt will ever be remembered for his simple and robust percussion revolvers, and the mass-production of these by machinery. Samuel Colt was born in 1814. After various enterprises he set about designing a simple but efficient revolver mechanism. It is thought that Colt saw and noted the complexity of the Collier flintlock revolver, and by 1835 his plans and models were sufficient for him to be granted an English patent and an American patent followed in 1836. The Colt Manufacturing Company was set up at Paterson, New Jersey in 1836 where the first of much sought after Paterson Colts were produced, in sizes that would be suitable for civilian and military use, from ·28 to ·44 calibre (plate 67). The success of this

Plate 68
Colt Walker-Whitney Dragoon revolver of ·44 calibre, dated 1847 on right hand side of the 9 inch barrel. Brass trigger guard.

venture depended on large government orders, so when, apart from minor orders, these were not forthcoming, he was obliged to close down at Paterson in 1843.

However those revolvers that had been used by the military proved most effective, and Captain Walker of the United States Dragoons stationed in Texas, having been impressed with the Paterson model, came to Colt and suggested a heavier military model. The result of their co-operation was the ·44 Colt made with the aid of Eli Whitney in 1847. This rare model is usually termed the Walker-Whitney Colt (plate 68).

Further government contracts followed, brought on by the war with Mexico and the growing demands of the great expansion westwards, so in 1848 Colt was able to establish his own factory at Hartford Connecticut. Here a variety of models were made: some 21,000 of the ·44 Dragoons or Old Army model with its round barrel, were produced up to the early 1860s when it was replaced by the New Army model. Large numbers of the 1848 and 1849 ·31 Pocket models (plate 69) were produced, particularly the latter, some 11,000 of which were produced at the London factory between 1853 and 1859. Also made in large numbers was the octagonal barrelled ·36 Navy pattern revolver of 1851 (colour plate 16), some 40,000 being made at the London factory.

Various other percussion models followed but in 1868 some were converted to take rim fire cartridges and these were followed in 1873 by the famous Single Action Army model, known as the Frontier model or 'Peacemaker'. Double-action cartridge models, were brought out in 1877 when the Colt Lightning appeared, and in 1878 the double-action was applied to the Army model.

In the late 1860s the English hunter and soldier H. A. Leveson on a hunting trip in and around the Rocky Mountains described the hunters, trappers and backwoodsmen he met: 'As a rule these are men of indomitable bravery, who in the pursuit of their dangerous calling carry their lives in their hands, and constantly owe their escape from their Indian enemies to their cool intrepidy, promptitude of action and skill with the rifle. Fine, tall, sinewy athletic fellows these solitary hunters are; and, although somewhat taciturn and reticent to a stranger, they are boon companions when their confidence is gained, and men of

107

sterling metal in a fray. Their usual costume is a fringed leather hunting-shirt, buckskin breeches, leggings and moccasins; and their armament is a heavy single small-bore rifle, a brace of revolvers and a Bowie knife. Their equipment consists of a saddle horse and two or three mules to carry packs containing reserve ammunition, a few pounds of tobacco, traps and pelts.'

The rifle would probably be of the percussion Kentucky type, the revolvers Colts and the Bowie knife, the workmanlike broad bladed knife named after its originator, Colonel Bowie, killed in the defence of the Alamo, Texas in 1836. The Bowie knife became very popular as a general service hunting and fighting knife and was made in great numbers in America and England, some being elaborately etched with patriotic slogans and designs. Early originals are desirable but they have been much imitated.

There were of course apart from Colt revolvers, also numerous others by Merwin Hulbert & Co, Remington and Smith and Wesson, there were many pepper box pistols and rifles such as Cochran's horizontally revolving turret rifle of 1837.

Most important, in that it led to the development of the famous Winchester repeating rifle, was Walter Hunt's 'Volitional Repeater' of 1849 in which his patent primed bullets were fed to the breech by a coil spring loaded tubular magazine which fitted under the barrel.

The invention by Benjamin Henry in 1860 of a ·44 rimfire metalic cartridge and other adjustments greatly improved the rifle, which became known as the Henry rifle. Nelson King's side gate loading system of 1866 further improved it and the rifle was then named the Winchester after the president of the company (plate 72 upper and middle).

Also about the same time the Spencer repeating rifle (plate 72 lower) had been developed, with a magazine in the butt, however, as this only held seven cartridges against the fifteen of the Winchester, and as the hammer had to be cocked each time, it was not able to compete successfully.

Plate 69
Engraved Colt Model 1849 Pocket pistol, 6 inch barrel, ·31 calibre. Cased in a London style case with all accessories.

108

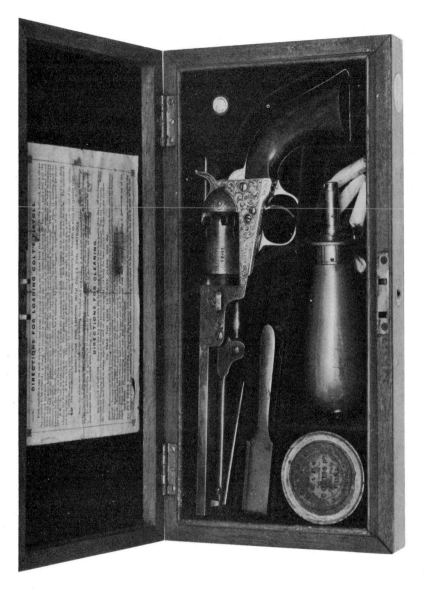

109

The Winchester repeater achieved tremendous popularity, being ideally suited to the needs of the frontier, and has been described as the rifle that won the West. The Winchester Repeating Arms Company brought out a second model in 1873, in which the well-known brass frame was replaced by iron. Also this 1873 model was designed for a longer centre fire cartridge and was manufactured in numerous varieties and calibres.

The years after the Civil War of 1861–5 saw the scramble westwards: land grabbing, gold seeking, railway building, the rise of the cattlemen, cowboys, gambling saloons, buffalo hunting, Indian wars, gunfighting, lawmen and the beginning of the legend of the West. The legend itself may well be said to date from the meeting in 1869 of William Cody and the journalist Edward C. Judson, who wrote under the name of 'Ned Buntline'. Cody's adventures were made the basis for a serial titled 'Buffalo Bill, King of the Border Men'. Cody was persuaded in 1872 to play in a stage version of Buntline's blood and thunder stories, but soon decided to branch out on his own with his famous Wild West Show.

Buffalo Bill's Wild West Show toured the world, two command performances were given in London for Queen Victoria in the year of her Jubilee 1887 and they returned to London in 1892 and 1903. There were displays of riding, roping and marksmanship and attacks by Indians on the Deadwood mailcoach. Fact and fiction soon became interwoven: the romanticising of the West had begun. Among the characters that Buffalo Bill persuaded to join his show in 1885 was 'Sitting Bull's a chief of the Sioux who with Crazy Horse and his braves surrounded and annihilated General Custer and the seventh Cavalry at the battle beside the Little Big Horn river in 1876. George Armstrong Custer was apparently determined to achieve glory at any cost; he finally put vanity before caution, causing the death of the 250 men under his command by rashly leading them into the Montana foothills, far in advance

Plate 70
Riding down a buffalo using a heavy calibre revolver.

of General Sheridan's main forces. Many of the Sioux and Cheyenne were armed with repeating weapons in addition to the Sharps rifles and carbines which were popular in the Civil War. Sitting Bull used a 1866 model Winchester.

One of the big attractions of Buffalo Bill's show from 1876 was Annie Oakley, the remarkable girl from Greenville, Ohio, who achieved great fame with her shooting act. Her early use of a Henry repeater followed by her later displays of rapid marksmanship with Winchesters did much to popularise these rifles (plate 74). Annie Oakley for all her prowess seems to have remained pleasantly feminine, with her long flowing curls and embroidered fringed skirt. She had the distinction of being presented to Queen Victoria and many other notable people but she seems to have remained charmingly modest in spite of all. Charles Lancaster, the English gunmaker, made shot guns for Annie when she was in England in 1887 and she also practised at 'clay pigeons' on Lancaster's shooting ground. She was given the name 'Little Sure Shot' when made a blood brother of the Sioux.

We now come to the aspects of the Western legend dealing with outlaws, gamblers, 'lawmen' and killers who roamed the cattle towns like predatory creatures. Some of these men have been romanticised out of all recognition but fortunately, for those who care to seek the truth, there exist some most revealing photographs that at a glance strip the legend bare. The true histories of the folk heroes of the West are available and read very differently from some of the popular versions. However there is a certain interest in just who of this motley lot

Plate 71
Fine quality English Bowie knife made for the American market by Edward Barnes and Sons, Sheffield. Blade etched with patriotic mottoes. Mid 19th century.

112

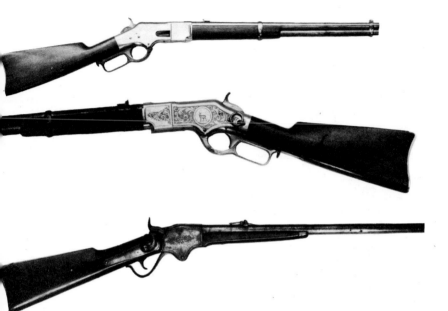

Plate 72

Upper: Winchester model 1866, brass
framed ·44 rimfire, lever action carbine.

Middle: Winchester model 1866, engraved
with nickel-plated frame, ·44 rimfire with
20 inch barrel. Butt trap contains 3 piece
rod, *circa* 1877.

Lower: Spencer ·56 rimfire repeating rifle,
26 inch barrel. First patented 1860.

113

Plate 73
American embossed 'Peace' powder flask,
with Eagle and clasped hands.

were fastest on the draw, or the most accurate and deadly killers, and in the guns they used.

William H. Bonney, later known as Billy the Kid, born in Brooklyn in 1859 had a typical delinquent case history. He ran away from home at the age of twelve when his mother married again in New Mexico, became a cowhand at Lincoln on the Pecos river and got mixed up with a local blood feud. After killing numerous men he put himself completely outside even the free and easy frontier law by killing the Sheriff of Lincoln and his deputy. He was hunted down and shot through the heart by Sheriff Pat Garrett in 1881. One of Bonney's guns was

114

Plate 74 Advertisement for Buffalo Bill's Wild West Show.
Annie Oakley with her Winchester repeating rifle.

115

a ·41 calibre, short-barrelled, double-action Colt but he doubtless used others, he seems to have been a pretty nasty type who
enjoyed killing his twenty-one victims, and but for his rather
catchy name he would probably not have been romanticised in
story and film.

Particularly popular with frontier outlaws was the ·45 calibre
Colt Peacemaker. An ivory handled Peacemaker is said to have
been used to shoot down Jesse James who was declared an out-
law for his part in fighting with the notorious Quantrell's
guerillas. From there he took to bank and train robbing until
killed for the reward money by members of his own gang.

Wyatt Earp seems to have been one of the coolest and most
calculating of the frontier gunmen, and also seems to have been
more or less on the side of the law, such as it was. He was noted

Plate 75
Henry Deringer's original pistol, percussion
with back action lock stamped DERINGER
PHILADEL. First introduced in the 1830s.

Colour plate 17
Cossack pistols.

Plate 76
Remington double deringer with over and
under rifled ·41 calibre barrels. Rimfire
cartridge. Estimated 150,000 manufact-
tured between 1866 and 1935.

for the calm and deadly way he made every shot tell rather
than a flashy quick draw, and the fact that he was one of the
few that survived to die with his boots off, suggests that there
was something to be said for this policy. Associated with Wyatt
Earp and his brothers Morgan and Virgil was the dentist who
turned to gambling, drinking and gunfighting, Doc Holliday.
These four were concerned in the controversial gunfight at the
O.K. Coral in Tombstone, Arizona in 1881, in which all four
of the McLowry gang were killed, and Morgan Earp was
wounded. Doc Holliday is said to have used a nickel plated
Peacemaker while Wyatt Earp certainly used Peacemakers too,
he doubtless used other types.

James Butler Hickok, born at Troy Grove, Illinois in 1837,

better known as Wild Bill Hickok, certainly lived up to his name. While working as a Wells Fargo stagecoach driver in Nebraska he shot the local Pony Express agent and two of his friends. Later he took to gambling and buffalo hunting, and during the short time he was Marshall of Abilene he accidentally shot his deputy in a gunfight over a game of cards. When Marshal of Hay City, Kansas he became involved in a brawl with soldiers of the 7th Cavalry, killing three and wounding nine. He was himself wounded and had to flee to avoid being taken by a cavalry detachment sent to bring him in dead or alive. Very much a dandy with an eye for the dance hall girls, he was finally shot in the back during a poker game at Deadwood City in 1876. He used a variety of guns including an English ·45 Adams, a Colt Dragoon, a pair of 1851 Navy pattern Colts with a pair of Deringers as secondary armament, and finally favoured the ·44 Smith and Wesson.

The Deringer pistol that could be carried unobtrusively, became one of the most popular personal protection weapons of the frontier. The original Deringer (plate 75) was a short-barrelled muzzle-loading pistol with a back action percussion lock and curled 'bird head' butt. These pistols in various sizes, mostly of moderate quality, were made by Henry Deringer, a Philadelphia gunsmith, from the 1830s. Deringer's name eventually came to be used to describe the type of gun, especially after the notoriety and publicity it received as the weapon used by John Wilkes Booth to assassinate President Abraham Lincoln in 1865. Apart from muzzle loading imitations which pirated the name, the term deringer was later applied to the cartridge models manufactured by Colt, and the popular double over and under barrelled pistol manufactured by Remington (plate 76). Favourite weapons of the gambling fraternity these deadly little pistols terminated the luck of many a gambling man.

5. Weapons of the Near East

The weapons to be described in this chapter come from lands that include North Africa, the Balkans, Turkey, Arabia, Syria, the Caucasus and all the lands eastwards as far as Mongolia and India.

For as long as history has been written these lands have seen the rise and fall of great empires, and across them the tides of conquest have ebbed and flowed.

Here after the ancient Assyrian and Egyptian empires had fallen, Alexander of Macedonia, in the third century B.C., led his army from Greece to India. Conquering Asia Minor, Syria and Egypt on the way, he then defeated the mighty army of Darius, ruler of the Persian Empire and continued his conquests into India. Alexander's victories were largely gained by his strong holding force of infantry that enabled him to exploit brilliantly the mobility of his cavalry. The inspired use of cavalry was to be the key to the success of the Arab conquests of the seventh and eighth century animated by the early zeal of their Mohammedan faith. In particular the light cavalry of Jenghis Khan, the Mongol Horde, in the thirteenth century was superbly organised and brilliantly led. These Mongol

119

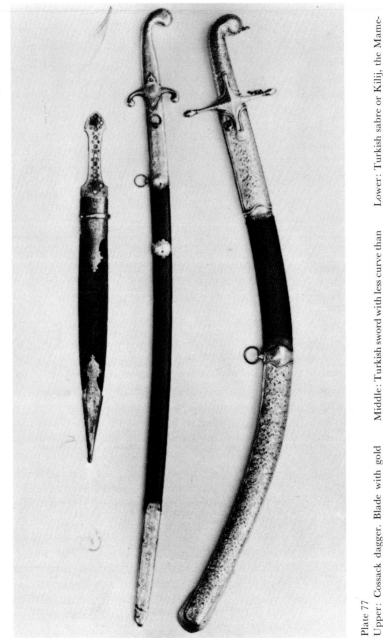

Plate 77

Upper: Cossack dagger. Blade with gold inlay, hilt with horn grips, scabbard velvet with steel mounts.

Middle: Turkish sword with less curve than usual. Hilt and scabbard mounts are silver with Turkish silver marks.

Lower: Turkish sabre or Kilij, the Mameluke style hilt and scabbard mounts of engraved silver.

horsemen carried a hooked lance, a curved scimitar, a lariat and the famous laminated tartar bow, in sizes suited to use from the saddle or on foot; they travelled light and lived off the country.

The fourteenth, fifteenth and sixteenth centuries saw the expansion of the Ottoman Turks. These semi-nomadic tribes of Asiatic origin, while being pressed from the east by the Mongols, expanded westwards first into Asia Minor, and then onwards until, by the mid-sixteenth century, the Balkans and Hungary were in their grip and they besieged Vienna. Constantinople had fallen in 1453 and the decaying Arab Empire had succumbed. The Mamelukes were defeated at Dabik in Syria in 1516 and a second victory in 1517 enabled the Turks to enter Cairo. From Egypt they proceeded to take parts of Arabia and North Africa as far as Algeria, where the foremost Barbary pirate, Khairredin Barbarossa was induced to give his allegiance to Selim I.

The Turks made great use of their highly trained infantry named Janissaries as well as their great numbers of cavalry including their elite cavalry, the Spahis. The Janissaries' original weapon was the short but powerful composite bow that had an effective fighting range of 200 to 300 yards. However as soon as practical firearms became available these were adopted, and incidentally great use was made of heavy cannon in such sieges as that of Constantinople. As secondary weapons the Janissaries carried sabres and daggers and a variety of weapons were used by them from time to time and also by the irregular infantry, such as the Bashibazouks. The cavalry were armed with the bow, lance and sword. After their great conquests the discipline and efficiency of their armies began to decline and they failed to keep abreast of developments in Europe.

Even this very brief sketch of the history of the area described will serve to illustrate the reason for the widespread occurrence of similar types of weapon over the whole area and in particular the weapons used by the lightly armed and armoured cavalry.

It is possible that the straight two-edged broad bladed Georgian type of dagger and that of the Cossacks (plate 77 upper) have derived from the short straight sword of the Romans. What is particularly interesting about some of the Cossack daggers of this type is the pattern welded strip of

121

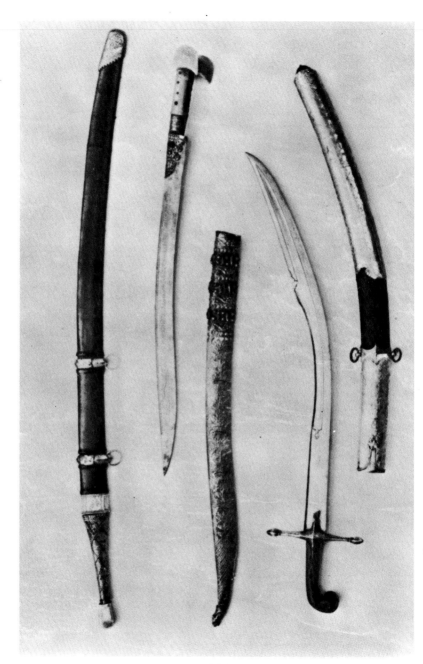

122

alternate twisted iron and steel that forms the middle of the blade. This could be a late survival of the forging method used in early European blades.

The Arab Jambiya (colour plate 18), a dagger having a broad curved blade with a central ridge, is found in modified versions in countries from North Africa to Persia and from Western India to East Africa. The shapes of the hilts and scabbards show considerable variation but the blade shape is basically the same.

Before firearms were adopted the powerful composite Tartar bow with its graceful curves was carried by horsemen in a sheath behind the saddle, together with a flat leather quiver for the arrows. This together with a lance, sword and round shield formed the equipment of the fighting horsemen. The curved sabre, designed to be used with a slashing cut, was also widely used. Some of these sabres have plain flat sided blades while others have a blade that both curves and broadens towards the tip; of these some have a distinct thrusting point, sometimes strengthened by a ridge. It is very difficult to lay down any hard and fast rules for discovering the place of origin of a sword from this area because not only were many of the best blades made in Persia and then mounted in different styles according to the country to which they were exported, but also the Turks for instance adopted the Mameluke style hilt in many of their later swords (plate 78). Persian and Turkish blades may be found in Polish and Hungarian sabres and as a result of Napoleon's Egyptian campaign in 1798 many French officers adopted the Mameluke style sabre. The fashion spread

Plate 78
Upper: Arab sword, interlaced silver wire hilt with no guard. These swords are often straight bladed.
Middle: Turkish Yataghan, showing typical blade shape and the distinctive hilt with large walrus ivory 'ear' pieces. Metal cased scabbard with repoussé designs and bands of turquoise, coral and malachite.
Lower: Turkish Kilij with fine blade of typical shape. Mameluke style hilt, quillons and scabbard mounts silver gilt.

123

Plate 79
Persian dagger *circa* 1800 with watered steel blades that divide into two or fit together so perfectly that the joins are difficult to see. Insides of the hilt damascened in gold.

124

until this style of sword was eventually adopted for General Officers of the British Army. Persian hilts are finished with a curved back pommel, sometimes in the shape of an animal's head, the quillons are straight and curve to a point at the centre, down over the blade and up over the grip. The typical Turkish sabre or kilij (plate 78 lower) is shorter and finished with more

Plate 80
North African style miquelet lock with silver inlay.

of a thrusting point than the extremely curved Persian shamshir.

There are however some distinctive types of sword, perhaps the most interesting and unusual being the Turkish Yataghan (plate 78 middle) with its slightly 'S' curved single-edged blade and hilt finished with large curled ivory grips. The Arab sword (plate 78 upper) found in parts of Arabia, East Africa and North East Africa is remarkable for its simple hilt bound with interlaced metalic strapwork with a square sectioned iron pommel and no guard or quillons; the blades are usually straight, in the style of European broadsword blades.

Of all the swords and daggers in this area, those with fine blades of 'watered' steel are most to be desired by the collector, and when these are further enriched with inscriptions inlaid in gold in beautiful Islamic scripts, they must certainly rank amongst the finest swords in the world.

At this stage it would be well to explain something of the fascinating history and method of making the steel from which the blades, generally known as Damascus, were forged. When in 327 B.C., Alexander the Great invaded India, he received as tribute quantities of a steel, so highly prized as to make an appropriate present to a great warrior. Indian steel ingots of this type were prepared in the Nirmal district of Hyderabad and exported to Syria and Persia. The Roman Emperor Diocletian (A.D. 245–313) founded armament factories at Damascus, which achieved a great reputation for fine weapons. In later years 'Damascus' came to be used as a general term to describe blades made from Indian steel.

In 1399 Tamerlane, founder of the Mughal Dynasty in India, conquered Syria and carried off the skilled workmen from Damascus setting them up in a new arms centre in Ispahan, Persia. There were also other notable centres of arms production at Khorassan and Samarkand on the trade routes across Asia. Large numbers of blades of the highest quality were produced in Persia from whence they were spread by trade and conquest as far as Morocco in the West and India in the East. Through Turkey they came to be used and prized in Hungary, and Poland. Then the major European armies adopted cavalry, uniformed and equipped in the style of Hungarian Hussars in the latter part of the eighteenth and early nineteenth century.

126

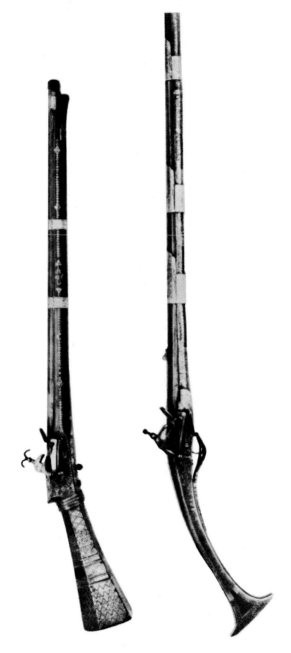

Plate 81

Upper: Typical Turkish style gun with miquelet lock, ball trigger and Damascus barrel. Profusely inlaid stock. *Circa* 1800.

Lower: Balkan gun with 48 inch barrel with engraved muzzle, miquelet lock and engraved iron butt.

127

Plate 82
Turkish Damascus twist barrel mounted on
an 18th century pistol.

The cakes of steel produced at Hydrabad were known in Western Europe as wootz. The structure of this metal is inherent in the ingot and not, as is the case with 'Damascus' barrels, of both Eastern and Western manufacture, composed of rods of alternate iron and steel twisted and welded together.

Briefly the method used to make the wootz cakes was firstly to take pieces of partially smelted high quality iron, place them

128

in sealed crucibles with carbonaceous material and heat them until the carbon combined with the iron, lowering its melting point sufficiently for it to become molten. This carbon iron, being too brittle to work, was broken up, coated with clay, heated almost to melting point and subjected to an air blast to burn away the excess carbon from the outside of each piece. The resulting billet, fuzed together, was then heated, forged out, folded and forged again a number of times until the carbon metal or globular cementite became spread in fine traceries throughout the low carbon metal or pearlite. This structure

Plate 83
Signed Turkish Damascus twist barrel with gold inlay, mounted on an 18th century pistol, later converted to percussion.

though somewhat difficult to forge, especially if the carbon content was rather high, was immensely strong and durable. Also because it was composed of very hard grains embedded in a strong binding material it was possessed of great cutting ability.

When the blade had been forged and polished the structure of the metal was exposed by immersing the blade in the acids of fruits. The pearlite is revealed by the darker streaks while the harder globular cementite is shown as a pattern like silvery ripples. Poets before the time of Mahomet likened the pattern of the metal to 'the wind gliding over the water' or 'the trails left in the sand by tiny ants'.

The type of blade known as kirk narduban or Mahomet's Ladder is particularly interesting because of the bands of pattern that run across the blade at intervals. These were obtained by filing grooves across the blade at intervals when it

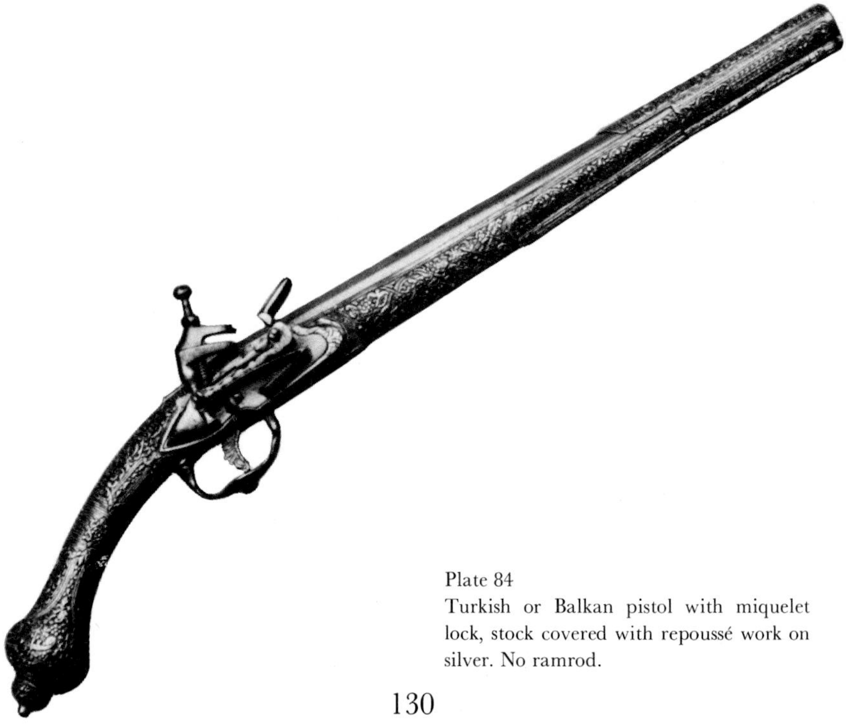

Plate 84
Turkish or Balkan pistol with miquelet lock, stock covered with repoussé work on silver. No ramrod.

130

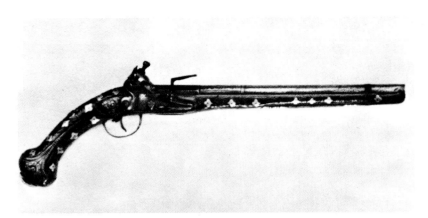

Plate 85
North African (Moroccan?) flintlock pistol
probably copied from a French or Italian
original. Steel mounts, stock inlaid with
silver. Dummy ramrod. *Circa* 1800.

was in a semi finished state and then the whole blade was
hammered flat again. These 'steps' then show the pattern of the
metal in depth, revealing the closely laid layers of carbon metal
resulting from the folding and forging stage. All swords and
daggers forged from this beautiful 'watered steel' should be
highly prized (plate 79).

In the fifteenth and sixteenth centuries when the Ottoman
Turks were pushing westwards into Eastern Europe and along
the North African coast, they were quick to adopt firearms and
soon excelled in making guns. The first being matchlock guns
of the arquebus type but by the middle of the seventeenth
century they had adopted the Mediterranean or Miquelet lock
(plate 80), which in variously modified forms spread around
the Mediterranean coasts and also to the Caucasus and Persia.

An exception is to be found in Algeria where the large Dutch
snaphaunce lock was more popular. Gun locks and guns were
originally important trade items which the Dutch exchanged
for exotic eastern goods with the merchants of the Barbary
Coast. Later skilfully made native copies of these locks replaced
the originals for use with the typical Algerian gun or rifle, with
its long slender barrel bound to the stock by many bands of
brass, iron or silver, and with the characteristic wide fishtail

131

butt. These graceful guns may be seen unchanged in the romantic pictures of North African tribesmen painted by Eugène Delacroix in the mid nineteenth century.

The typical Turkish gun (plate 81 upper) changed little from the overall shape of a European matchlock, being only slightly modified. The stock is stepped down behind the breech for the thumb, and the butt is heavy with flat sides, often richly inlaid. A notable feature of the Turkish gun is the use of a small ball trigger without a guard. Also of great interest are the finely forged twist barrels to be found on many Turkish guns (plate 82). These were either forged from ribbons composed of alternate iron and steel strips wound round a mandril and forged together with the edges of the strips to the outside of the barrel, or they were made from rods of alternate iron and steel, which were first twisted before being wound round the mandril. The beauty of the metal is usually shown by deep etching with acid and they are sometimes further enriched with gold inlay (plate 83). Such was the fame of these barrels that they are often to be found finely mounted in European arms. They are most desirable collectors' items.

Another distinctive type of gun with a miquelet lock comes

Plate 86
Typical short Turkish blunderbuss, the stock carved and inlaid with silver wire, the style of decoration showing European influence. Barrel chiselled with decoration at the breech. Early 19th century.

from the Balkans, often attributed to Albania (plate 81 lower). It is remarkable for an exceptionally slender butt curving downwards with a great degree of bend, flaring slightly towards its narrow, straight heel plate. The pistols too from this area are interesting for their slender shape and for being almost covered with repoussé patterned brass or silver (plate 84).

A characteristic feature of almost all Balkan and eastern pistols is their lack of a ramrod; this was worn tucked in the sash and attached to a cord together with a pricker and small flask. This was a sensible arrangement for the rod could not be lost in the heat of battle, one rod could serve two pistols and because it did not have to be withdrawn and replaced each time, loading was made quicker. Some Balkan and North African pistols are copies of fine French and Italian pistols but can be recognised by the curious practice of carving dummy ramrods into the stock (plate 85).

Perhaps the most desirable type of pistol from this whole area is the slender Cossack pistol from the Caucasus (colour plate 17); it is probable that some of the finest were made in Persia. These pistols have a miquelet type of lock and small ball triggers. The slender stocks are covered with leather and bound to the barrel by bands of silver decorated with niello inlay. Often the locks and barrels are damascened in gold and the butt is finished with a large ivory ball. Niello is a black alloy of sulphur, lead, silver and copper and was much used for inlay on silver or gold on fine Cossack weapons, particularly the typical Cossack straight bladed dagger. Some of the finest of the Cossack daggers and pistols bear the name of the same maker struck onto a gold inset on the blade and lock plate respectively.

A blunderbuss with a short flared barrel and short stock was a favourite weapon which was widely used in North Africa, the Balkans and Turkey (plate 86).

A number of battle axes and maces were used by the Persians and Turks the most unusual being the bull-head mace of the Persians.

There is still much to be discovered about the weapons covered by this chapter so a collector will have opportunities for original research.

Colour plate 20
Akbar Shar.

Plate 87
Two decorative Indian Katars.

134

6. Weapons of India and Indonesia

India like the Near East suffered waves of invasion and looting. Of the conquering armies that marched over the Hindu Kush and through the famous Kyber Pass into the fertile plains of Hindustan, most conquered, looted and returned whence they had come. Alexander and his Macedonian-Greek army, between 327–5 B.C., conquered and departed. Numerous raids were made into India by the nomadic tribes of central Asia, one of the most powerful invasions being that of Timur the Mongol, who in 1398 sacked Delhi, before retiring to his capital Samarkand.

The Mughal dynasty that was to have a profound effect on the arts, culture and the weapons of India, began as a result of a series of limited conquests and settlements from the tenth to the sixteenth century. By 1530 Babur the Tiger had laid the foundations for the Mughal Empire that was to be inherited by his grandson Akbar the Great. By his skill as a general and administrator Akbar consolidated his Empire, then proceeded to enrich it by encouraging the arts, drawing to his court some of the greatest artists, craftsmen, poets and philosophers from Persia and Hindustan. As a result of his enlightened rule, the cultures of Persia and Hindustan intermingled, and so far as weapons are concerned, this relationship can be traced in all those arms generally classified as Indo-Persian.

The early Mughal conquests resulted from the skilled direction of large armies of highly mobile mounted archers, typical of those that proved so effective on the steppes of Asia. However as the Turko-Islamic conquerors settled in India they adopted some of the local weapons and warriors into their armies, including Indian infantry using their traditional bows, spears and swords, four wheeled chariots carrying archers or spearmen and also the mighty war elephants that were used in large numbers in traditional Hindu armies.

From the late fourteenth and fifteenth centuries, guns were brought to India by the invaders. By the early sixteenth century Babur was making considerable use of both matchlock guns and cannons.

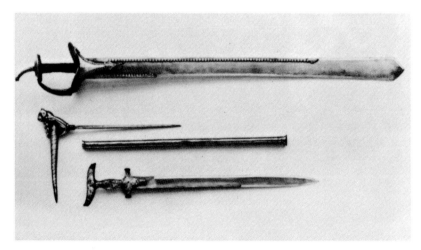

Plate 88
Upper: Khanda, favourite sword of the Rajput and Mahratta cavalry. The iron hilt decorated with foliated engravings.
Middle: Combined spike axe and dagger of crutch type, said to have been used by Fakirs.
Lower: Small crutch sword with hilt damascened in gold and silver.

Plate 89
Detail of Indo-Persian knife blade showing
watered steel and signature of maker,
'work of Taqi'.

Having looked at the general picture, we will first examine
some of the traditional weapons found in India and then go on
to deal with those produced as a result of the Mughal conquests.

The most widely used sword was the tulwar with its curved
single-edged flat sided blade and iron hilt. The characteristic
feature of the hilt is the round iron pommel topped with an
ornamental cone. A knuckle guard extends from the quillon
to the outer edge of the pommel. The blades of these swords
can vary from fine watered steel to the commonest sort,
and the hilts can be richly damascened with gold or rather
thinly with silver. The scabbards of the finest are often of silk
velvet and the mounts gold damascened. A favourite weapon
of the Rajput and Mahratta cavalry was the khanda (plate 88),
which may be described as a heavy cavalry sword akin to the
European broadsword. The blade is strongly reinforced towards the hilt and widens towards the tip. The hilt is a stronger,
bigger and more elaborate version of the tulwar type of hilt
and the inside of the guard and knuckle-bow is usually lined
with velvet.

Particularly associated with the famous cavalry of the
Mahrattas is the straight bladed gauntlet-sword called a pata.

137

Plate 90
Indian dagger with strengthened back rib and diamond sectioned armour piercing point. Detail showing fine watered steel blade with chiseled decoration and gold inlay, including signature. Persian influence in decoration.

The flexible blade resembles a European broadsword blade, and in fact many were of European origin. The iron gauntlet which is attached to the blade, covers the fist and forearm; the fist being clenched round a bar for thrusting.

The katar (colour plate 21), a straight bladed dagger which is also designed to be used with a punching thrust, was popular with the Mahrattas and Rajputs; it was widely adopted by the Mughal conquerors.

Associated with the warlike tribes of the North West Frontier of India is the workmanlike kyber knife with its broad

138

straight blade tapering to a strong tip. The tang forms the
backbone of the hilt onto which ivory grips are riveted. These
kyber knives can vary in size and quality considerably, the
finest having 'watered' steel blades, and the iron parts of the
hilts richly damascened with gold. There is also a dagger with a
blade of a slight 'S' shape curving to a finely tapered tip of
diamond section. This wicked looking point was designed for

Plate 91
Left to right: Indian jambiya with watered
steel blade, iron hilt damascened with gold.
 Indian jambiya with watered steel panels,
chiseled and damascened designs and ivory
hilt.
 Indian all steel dagger or Chilanum,
used by the Mahrattas. Typical grooved
blade.
 Indian dagger with gilt blade and hilt.

piercing chain mail.

The weapons from Nepal are of particular interest for they include the well-known kukri knife retained as a service weapon by the renowned Gurkha Rifles. The sheath of the kukri also has provision for a small knife and a steel of a similar shape to the main knife; a third compartment contains a simple leather wallet. Another type of Nepalese sword, the korah, has a straighter blade than the kukri until it curves and broadens at the tip. The hilt has a circular guard and pommel; a stylised lotus flower is usually found inlaid in the broad end of the blade.

A strong combined sword and bush knife was used by the Coorgs of S. W. India. This curiously shaped knife has some resemblance to the kukri but the blade is broader and the cutting edge mostly straight; the hilt of carved ivory has a long tapered flat sided pommel.

Various types of battle axe were widely used, one of the most interesting of these being the 'crow-bill' headed axe common in the Cutch area. As its name suggests its head is finished with a sharply pointed beak-like shape, and it often has a thin dagger screwed into the end of the haft. Various types of mace were also used.

The crutch sword (plate 88) kept by rajahs beside their divans served both as an arm rest and a handy weapon in the

Plate 92

Left: A fine mutton fat jade Khanjar hilt of scroll form set with emeralds and rubies, the former carved as vine leaves and bunches of grapes, the rubies as Lotus flowers and buds. Mughal, 18th century.

Centre: A fine Indian Khanjar with watered steel blade and celadon jade hilt of scroll form set with emeralds, rubies and diamonds, arranged in a pattern of flowers and foliage joined with branches of sunken gold. Mughal, 18th century.

Right: Fine Javanese gold kris hilt in the form of a demon, set with rubies, sapphires and a carbuncle. The base set with foiled crystals and a cat's-eye. Early 19th century.

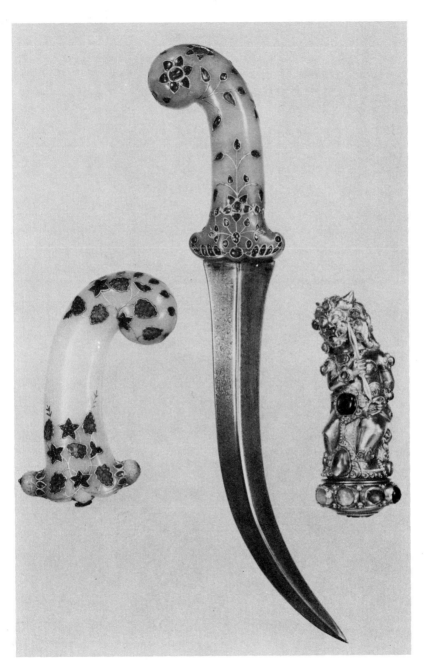

141

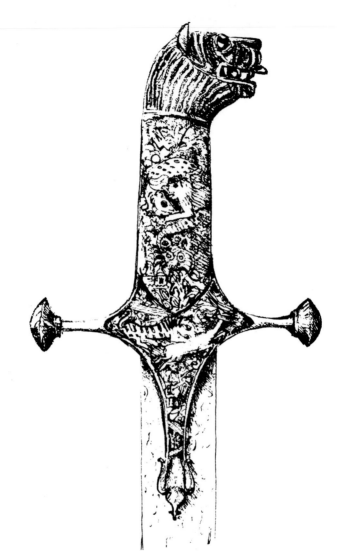

Plate 93
Sabre with fine watered steel blade and
tiger headed hilt damascened with gold
designs of animals. Scabbard iron of
regulation army type, also damascened
with gold. Probably made for a British
officer, early 19th century.

142

event of surprise attack. The finest of these have the crutch hilt carved in jade.

Interesting are the parrying shields made from antelope horns, the points being at opposite ends and sometimes there is a small round shield in the middle. The steel tipped points of the horns could of course be used offensively. Unusual weapons include the chakram or sharp-edged steel quoit carried by the Sikhs of the Punjab in their conical turbans. These were thrown by twirling them round the first finger thereby imparting a spinning motion to them and increasing the cutting action of the edge when it stuck.

Weapons associated with assassination were a dagger named the bichwa or scorpion's sting and the vicious baghnak or 'tiger's claw'; these were steel claws gripped in the clenched fist with the first and fourth finger through iron rings.

Characteristic of Indo-Persian weapons is the intermingling of the types of weapon and styles of decoration of each. The most desirable of the Mughal weapons are undoubtedly those with the hilts superbly carved in jade of various colours and

Plate 94
Beaumont-Adams percussion revolver *circa* 1858, damascened all over with floral designs in gold.

143

Plate 95
Fine example of a laminated Javanese
blade. Enlarged detail of sword in plate 97.

blades gracefully forged and shaped, sometimes with chiselled
ornament enriched with gold inlay. Hilts carved in the shape of
horses' or rams' heads were popular and are often very fine
examples of the jade carvers' art. Where the piece of jade has
particularly beautiful variations of colour it is best seen with
restrained carving. However, plain jade, particularly the
opaque white or 'mutton fat' jade was often enriched with

144

jewels inset with pure gold. Two fine examples of these hilts are illustrated, showing how sensitively the graceful form and decoration of the hilt has been integrated with the shape of the watered steel blade (plate 92).

The Mughal conquerors brought with them into India matchlock guns which derived from Turkish matchlocks. The most widespread and typical gun or toradar found in India had a simple match holder that moved forward onto the priming pan when the trigger was pressed up from below the butt. The butt, with its flat, straight sides, could not be more simple and has the abrupt step down behind the breech found in Turkish guns. The long barrel is bound to the slender stock with wire or bands and a pricker for cleaning the touch hole is often attached by a chain near the breech (colour plate 21).

The Afghan gun or rifle known as a jezail, has a slightly curved stock of oval section and often has a hinged two-prong barrel support. Matchlocks from the Sind area have an exceptionally curved butt which widens out into a long and narrow heel plate. These matchlocks continued to be made and used in the nineteenth century, a few only being fitted with European flintlocks.

Of particular interest are those matchlock guns fitted with 'Damascus' barrels, for some of these are of exceptional quality, often deeply etched to reveal the structure of the twisted metal. Also of course there are some finely enriched examples which are well worth collecting for their decorative qualities.

Some interesting weapons resulted from British rule in India particularly in the nineteenth century. Officers apparently had swords made in the Indo-Persian style, an example of which is shown (plate 93). The tiger head iron hilt is damascened in gold and the blade is of fine watered steel, but what suggests that this sword was made for a British officer is the typical regulation style iron scabbard, though this also is damascened all over with gold.

There are numbers of Colt and British revolvers, imported into India around 1850, that were finely damascened all over in gold (plate 94). Also many of the Indian princes had very fine quality sporting guns and rifles made by the top British makers. Characteristic of many of these, apart from their finish and the lavishly fitted cases, was the heavy gold plating

145

Plate 96
Javanese kris with stylised Garuda hilt carved in wood.

of the locks and all the iron furniture.

There is an interesting type of gun that comes from Ceylon which is unusual for its use of a form of miquelet lock, probably derived from Portuguese originals. Also it has a butt that ends in what could be described as a large curled fishtail or a large tendril form, enriched with carving. Also from Ceylon comes a curiously carved dagger and short curved sword that has a hilt finished in a fantastically stylised animal head.

The weapons of Indonesia have many interesting features,

some of the finest coming from Java and Bali where the most beautiful kris blades were forged.

Kris blades, whether straight or of the wavy kind, consist of laminations of iron and steel forge welded together. Not only did this method of forging make the blades stronger, but because of the manner in which the metal stratas were laid

Plate 97
Javanese sword with carved horn hilt and remarkable blade of intricate iron and steel laminations. See also plate showing detail of blade.

together, filed and forged out flat again, a great variety of decorative effects could be obtained. The effect was brought out and enhanced by prolonged etching with acid until the laminations attained a curious eaten away appearance (plate 95). Certain kris blades of exceptional quality are finished smooth and of a deep colour, the forging pattern being shown by a fine delicate silver tracery. Sometimes fine kris will have some gold inlay in the blade near the hilt and a gold ferrule between the hilt and blade, either carved or inset with jewels.

The hilts of many kris are more or less stylised versions of Garuda, the bird-like deity of Hindu mythology. In some versions, carved in wood or ivory, Garuda is represented as a wizened little man with a beak-like nose and folded arms, but in other versions the design has been formalised into an abstract shape, only vaguely resembling the general outline (plate 96). On exceptional examples, the Garuda or other deity, may be overlaid in sheet gold and set with precious or semi-precious stones (plate 96 right).

The scabbards of kris are also interesting for the big carved wood mouth often has a grain that rivals the figure of the blade, and the remainder of the scabbard can be sheathed in silver or gold, covered all over with delicate repoussé designs.

A less common type of heavier single-edged sword from Java is illustrated. This has a carved horn hilt and a remarkable blade composed of laminations of iron to which has been forge-welded further U-shaped laminations along the top of the blade (plate 97).

All fine examples of kris blades and their carved hilts are worthy collectors' items though they have not always fetched the prices they deserve.

7. Weapons of Japan

The weapons of Japan have many features that are unique, arising out of the style of fighting that developed during centuries of internal warfare when they were largely isolated from the outside world, or deliberately shunned outside influences. When at last Japan was abruptly thrown open to westernisation in the latter half of the nineteenth century, the weapons currently in use were of a type that had been traditional for centuries.

The invading ancestors of the Japanese had as a result of persistent fighting gradually forced the original inhabitants, the Ainu, into the island of Hokkaido in the north. Then they fought among themselves to settle which of the rival clans was to rule Japan. The internal wars became almost a national pastime relieved by short spells of peace or invasions of Korea. In 1274 and 1281 the Japanese had to use all their strength to repel the Mongol invasions launched by Kublai Khan and in this they were aided by storms that destroyed or scattered the Mongol fleet.

Most notable of the internal struggles was the 250 years of fighting between the Taira and the Minamoto. Finally,

Colour plate 22
Japanese battle by moonlight.

towards the end of the twelfth century, the Minamoto emerged victorious, led by their great general and swordsman, Yoshitsune. Minamoto Yoritomo being installed as shogun in 1192.

As in Asia the main offensive weapon of the mounted knight or Samurai was the bow, but the Japanese developed a particularly powerful bow of about 7 feet in length which was drawn back behind the ear. This composite bow was unusual in that its grip was well below mid-way. The long feathered arrow shafts were tipped with a variety of precisely shaped arrow-heads with hardened points. The bow remained popular into the nineteenth century in spite of the introduction of matchlock guns around the middle of the sixteenth century.

The mounted Samurai also carried in the slung position a long slightly curved sword termed a tachi and a dagger named a tanto (colour plate 24). The sword had a particular importance in Japan not only as a weapon but also because it symbolised the soul of the Samurai, faithful unto death in the service of his lord.

Early straight-bladed iron swords had come into Japan from China. Some early attempts at sword making had proved unsuccessful because of the liability of the blades to break or bend, but in the early years of the eighth century the great swordsmith Amakuni produced swords of a slightly curved type that were to remain more or less standard until the present. One of the most fascinating aspects of collecting Japanese swords is the fact that there is always a chance of coming across a very old blade, perhaps of the twelfth or thirteenth century, that may have been remounted in the nineteenth century or even for military use in the 2nd World War. There were notable periods of sword forging in the tenth and twelfth centuries leading to the era of the greatest swordsmiths in the thirteenth and fourteenth centuries. This was the era that was to give rise to the three swordsmiths considered by the Japanese to be the greatest of all: Yoshimitsu of Awataguchi, (1229–1291), Masamune of Sagami, (1264–1343) and his finest pupil Go Yoshihiro (1299–1325). By his example and through his pupils, the influence of Masamune had a tremendous and enduring effect on the art of the swordsmith. His blades had a functional fitness combined with a perfection of grace and proportion that remained unsurpassed.

150

Plate 98

Wakizashi blade by Tsuta omi no kami
Sukenao of Osaka in Setsu province. 17th
century. Signed tang and tip of blade
showing fine quality yakiba.

151

備後守□□道

152

In the sixteenth century, with the increase of fighting on foot when battles tended to develop into a series of fencing matches, a new style of sword was developed at Seki in Mino province. The Seki style of sword was shorter, straighter and stronger than the long, slender, curved tachi designed for fighting on horseback. In the seventeenth century wonderful blades suited to fighting on foot were forged at Osaka by renowned sword-smiths like Sukehiro, Sukenao (plate 98) and Shinkai notable for the quality and depth of the hardened edge or yakiba. The eighteenth century saw something of a decline in sword forging, in that there was a tendency to put the decorative effect of the yakiba before its functional purpose. However Suishinshi Masahide 1750–1825 revived the best of the old traditions in the fine blades he forged, but also he spread his ideas widely by writing some excellent books embodying his principles. As a result many blades of the finest quality were produced in the nineteenth century, worthy to be as highly prized as many of the older blades. Blades prior to 1600, it has been customary to designate Koto or old blades and after 1600, Shinto or new swords.

The typical Japanese sword has a slight to moderate curve, a single cutting edge and an angled cutting tip. The russet iron tang of the blade is important for it can suggest the age or origin of a blade, also it will often have engraved into it the signature of the swordsmith and perhaps his town and province. The other side of the tang is sometimes engraved with the date.

The blade may be divided into three main areas. The cutting edge and its hardened area, known as the yakiba, is distinguished by its frosted appearance. Above this frosted area, the outline of which is known as the hamon, there lies the part of the blade that shows the jihada or grain of the folded metal. Above this the shinogi or upper part of the blade is burnished mirror bright (plate 98). Apart from the general shape of the

Plate 99
Wakizashi blade of flat sided type by Tama no Kami Yoshimichi, *circa* 1600. Signed tang and blade tip showing fine mokume (wood grain) and unusual yakiba known as Sudari.

153

blade and its tang, the yakiba, hamon and the jihada are most important in identifying a blade, they represent the true 'signature' of a master smith (plate 99). The signature on the tang may be a courtesy signature by a pupil of the master or it may be a deliberate forgery. Any blade man worth his salt will be as pleased with a good unsigned blade as with one bearing an illustrious signature. However, it is a fact that a blade with a signature will fetch a higher price than an unsigned one, such is the naive faith in the characters on the tang. There is therefore a great opportunity for the discerning collector of blades to get some of the very best at a more reasonable price. The possibility of finding a very fine unsigned blade (colour plate 23) is made more likely because many of the great masters, particularly the earlier, did not sign their work, holding that anyone who could not recognise the work of a master did not deserve to know.

Although there were infinite numbers of minor variations, the general method of forging a blade using only the simplest means, a charcoal fire, hammers and an anvil was as follows. Iron of the purest quality was beaten out, folded and forge welded together about twelve times to make the iron for the softer inner core of the blade. The iron for the outer casing of the blade was folded and forged fifteen to twenty times.

Next the tough dense outer skin was folded round the inner core and forged out into the blade shape, the whole thoroughly hammered to condense the metal. When the blade had been filed up to shape, it was made ready for the vital water hardening process by covering the whole blade with a clay mixture. When dry this clay mixture was carefully scraped away along the blade edge in a manner which depended on the depth of yakiba and hamon required.

The blade was now evenly heated until white hot, the smithy being darkened so that the smith could judge the correct heat, and then after days of work came the moment that could

Plate 100
Tsuba of the 18th and 19th centuries showing something of the great variety of treatment and subject matter.

154

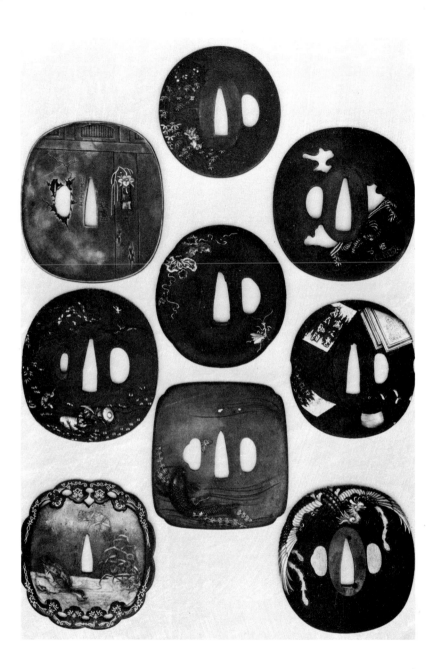

155

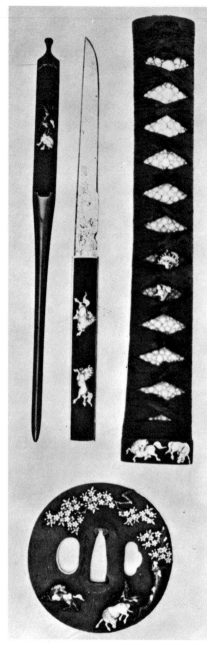

Plate 101
Left: Kogai by Goto Mitsutaka.
Middle: Kodsuka by Yanagawa Nagaharu.
Right: Sword hilt showing samé or ray
skin bound with silk cord over the menuki,
with kashira (top) and Fuchi (bottom) by
Omori Teruji.
   Lower: Tsuba by Nara Yoshinori.

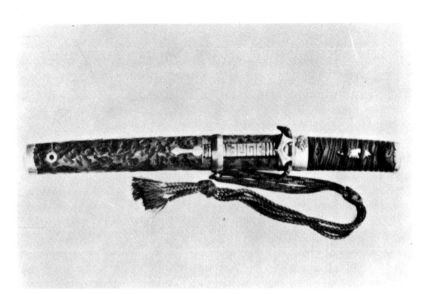

Plate 102
Yoroi-toshi, a dagger with a thick armour
piercing blade. Showing mounts fitted and
interesting decorative treatment of the
scabbard and the sageo or silk tying cord.

make or mar the blade. At white heat the blade was quickly
and smoothly plunged into a trough of luke warm water, the
exact temperature of which was a closely guarded secret. If all
was just right and all the preliminary forging had resulted in a
blade of even density and stress then a wonderful blade may
well emerge. However, if any one factor was amiss, a soft or
brittle, cracked or distorted blade would result. Forging a fine
blade was a test of dedicated concentration which reflected the
spirit of Zen Buddhism.

The blade was next handed over to a specialist polisher, who
with a series of twenty graded water stones and his various
papers gradually brought the blade to a scratchless finish in
such a way as to reveal the grain of the metal and the frosty
appearance of hardened yakiba. Where the hamon, or top edge
of the yakiba, has clusters of bright spots known as niye it is
usually an indication of a good blade.

A fine Japanese blade has a clean and functional shape

157

which is remarkably modern in appearance and it also has an awesome cutting ability. The hardened edge takes a razor sharpness, and the angled cutting tip or kissaki is particularly deadly.

A Samurai in civilian dress would carry the two swords that were his special privilege through his sash with the blade edge uppermost. The longer of these two swords is known as a katana and the shorter a wakizashi. From the seventeenth century onwards it was increasingly the custom to mount the blades with furniture that reflect the extraordinary skill and inventiveness of the Japanese metal-workers (plate 100).

Japanese sword mounts particularly of the seventeenth, eighteenth and nineteenth centuries often form the sole objects of a collector's interest. Their charm lies in the infinite invention of design and subject matter and in the extraordinary range of techniques employed.

The best known and most popular of sword fittings is the sword guard or tsuba. This generally has a circular shape but there are also many variations, and it will have in the centre a hole which coincides with the section of the blade to which it had been fitted.

Also interesting are the fuchi or collar and kashira on top of the hilt which were made as a pair and show differing aspects of the same subject matter. Between the ray skin and the silk binding of the hilt are found the menuki, little designs on either side of the hilt also having related subjects.

The kodsuka is a short knife which fits into a slot in the scabbard of a wakizashi and it sometimes has its companion the rarer kogai, a skewer-like object, fitted into a slot on the other side. There are also several scabbard mounts.

Even where a Japanese sword has suffered badly from damage or neglect there will often be some fitting of interest worth saving and often some design or technique that has not been seen by the collector before.

Plate 103
Three wakizashi (upper) and three katana (lower) showing a few of the infinite variety of mounts and the decorative treatments of the scabbards.

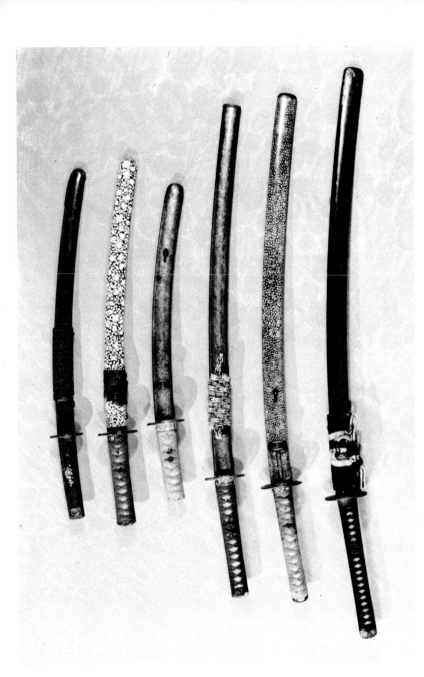

Of the metals used for sword fittings, iron, with its wide variety of forged and russet finishes, is one of the most subtle and interesting. Shakudo, which is a mixture of copper and gold, takes on rich blue-black patina. Shibuichi, a mixture of silver and copper, patinates to silvery greys. Copper patinates to soft reds. Also silver and various shades of gold were used.

In the earliest tsuba, which were almost all of iron, the decoration if any would be very simple, usually taking the form of cut-out shapes of some symbolic object or clan symbol.

These early pieces are by no means to be despised since the simplicity of design is complemented by skilful forging, hammer marks and subtle russet iron finishes which give a character to the best of these pieces, which can satisfy the matured collector, long after a tour de force in soft metal has lost its initial impact. In the seventeenth century the restrained designs of Goto metalworkers were popular for formal and court occasions; these were almost all of shakudo enriched with gold, national emblems and flowers dominating. Towards the end of this century the freer designs of the Nara school had a great influence, particularly attractive being those mainly forged in iron with details in soft metals.

The eighteenth and nineteenth centuries show the full flowering of the great variety of styles and schools of sword fittings, the techniques and designs of which show such amazing invention (plate 101). The subject may range from past battles with many tiny armoured figures in a landscape, to a single bold object superbly worked and placed to perfection: such is often the work of the great masters. Curious folk tales, stories from the past, illustrated sayings, deities and sages, symbolic birds, beasts, flowers, fish, insects, the moon, stars, clouds and waves might be modelled to an incredible degree of naturalism in patinated metals or formalized almost to abstraction.

Most of the later metalworkers signed their work but, as with sword blades, quality of design and workmanship should convince before the judgement is swayed by an illustrious signature, which may not always be by the hand of the master.

The ability to suggest so much in so small a space is a part of the appeal of sword fittings where a whole landscape, a storm, a waterfall and rushing river among the rocks may be conveyed

160

with the simplest of means. A famed story like the battle of Musashi-no is suggested by the wolf foraging among the bones in the long grass by the light of the full moon; and the story of revenge taken when gaining entry to a castle disguised as gardeners is shown by the billhooks lying on the blood-stained tiles.

Truly it may be said that to collect and study sword fittings is a charming way of discovering something of the history, the folklore and the natural history of Japan and gaining an appreciation of the Japanese genius for design.

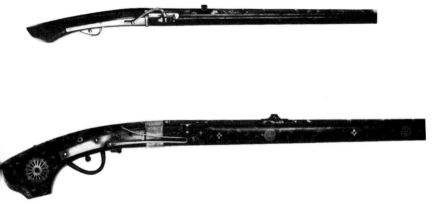

Plate 104
Upper: Typical Japanese matchlock gun with silver inlaid barrel.
Lower: Japanese matchlock gun with inlaid barrel and decoratively lacquered stock. Serpentine or matchcord holder missing.

161

Japanese pole-arms are well worthy of attention, some of the spear heads being finely forged and shaped. The curved glaive blades of the formidable naginatas were sometimes the work of good swordsmiths. Straight spear heads are occasionally found mounted as daggers. There are also some spear heads with a finely faceted cross piece. Spear heads and arrow heads have such clean graceful shapes as to place them very high as objects of functional beauty.

Traditionally firearms were introduced into Japan in 1543. The matchlock continued as the only lock until the middle of the nineteenth century (plate 104). However, Japanese matchlock guns are usually of good quality, the barrels being strong and precisely forged like all Japanese weapons. Often the barrels are inlaid with gold and silver designs and many were signed by the maker. The stock, which was often richly lacquered, had a simple curved butt which did not fit onto the shoulder; the considerable weight of the gun barrel taking the bulk of the recoil. Pistols look like small and rather stubby versions of the guns.

For the most part the use of firearms in battle was not considered to be in accordance with the warrior code, probably because it so easily brought to naught skill with sword, spear and bow.

Only in the campaign of Kawanakajima 1553–1563 were they widely used. One of the colour plates illustrates the frustration and hatred of Yamamoto Kansuke and his warriors as they are shot down by the musket fire of Takeda Shingen's troops (colour plate 24).

In the later half of the nineteenth century a few percussion pistols were made which are disguised as daggers, the pistol having a tanto hilt and the barrel fitting into a scabbard, from which it is drawn to be cocked and fired. The disguising of a firearm in this manner also suggests a reluctance to have their use openly known.

Japanese guns are now more highly thought of as collectors' items, those with fine barrels and pistols are particularly desirable.

162

8. Some hints on the restoration of weapons

It is most pleasant but alas increasingly rare to find weapons in perfect original condition, especially at the sort of price that an average collector can afford. There are however many occasions when a chance comes to buy a weapon that has suffered loss of parts or damage. The questions that a collector must decide are: in the first place can the weapon be fully restored to something approaching its former state, and secondly will the expense and labour be justified. The latter will depend on its rarity and interest and whether the same money could be better spent elsewhere.

However, assuming that the item is of particular interest, it then becomes a labour of love to restore it; expense and time become of less consequence.

It often occurs that a fine gun or pair of pistols are contained in a case, the inside compartments of which have suffered. Where moths have ravished the baize lining, a decision has to be made as to whether it can be carefully filled in with pieces from a similar old piece of baize pasted into the gaps. If moth and broken partitions cannot be repaired in a satisfactory way then the best thing is to remake and reline the inside of the case

163

completely with a material nearest to the original. The trade label should be carefully removed from the baize if possible, but if not, removed with the baize, neatly trimmed round with a sharp knife and rule and pasted or glued back onto the new cloth lining in the lid. Paper patterns pressed tightly into the corners of the case are a great help in getting a precise fit to the cloth lining and a stiff paste applied to the wood the best adhesive, for it is strong when dry but gives time for adjustment. It is perhaps as well to try one's skill at lining something like an old cigar box first, and if in doubt hand the job to a skilled man.

It is important to preserve any original finish, so if there is some slight surface rust on a pistol or gun, this should be carefully dealt with by working off the raised rust with a piece of copper which, because it is softer, will not scratch. Then a good rub with a rag and a light cleaning oil will complete the job, leaving intact what remains of the barrel browning, case hardening colour on the locks and charcoal blue on the furniture.

When all original finish has been lost it is then a matter of cleaning and polishing the surfaces of the metal with a combination such as Duraglit and jewellers' Diamantine. Emery paper on a wood block will of course be needed for deep rust. When the rust pitting has been stuck off the barrels, these will be much enhanced by having them well rebrowned, a process of controlled rusting that brings out the distinctive pattern of a twist or Damascus barrel. Normally it is best not to reblue trigger guards and certainly not with chemical blue or black, nor is it wise to re-case harden lock-plates.

The woodwork on guns or pistols may well need attention. First remove dirt, varnish and gun oil with suitable solvents; gun oil and grease in particular will give the wood a very dull look. Dents may be raised by damping the wood and applying a hot iron; other marks may be lightly rubbed down with a very fine abrasive and then the wood brought up with purified linseed oil. After several applications it can be given a very light coat, applied with a smooth rag, of a good gun-stock varnish, to help as a final finish but on no account should this be thickly applied.

All too often pistols have been the playthings of young boys, who have lost a ramrod or bullet mould or broken a cock,

then perhaps someone has borrowed the turnscrew. The collector finding pistols in this state faces the difficult problem of finding suitable replacements, making himself or having made, a ramrod, a new top jaw and screw for the cock, and so on. If this is well done it will considerably increase the desirability of the pair of pistols and therefore increase their value.

It is most important that gunmakers' turnscrews be used when stripping a gun or pistol. The slot in a gun screw is usually fine and deep, so a fine hollow ground turnscrew must be used. If an ordinary blunt screwdriver is used it will not fit deep enough to give a good grip and an ugly broken screw slot may result. A sharp tap on the top of a turnscrew may loosen a screw lightly rusted in.

Good quality guns are a joy to take to pieces but great care must be exercised to avoid scratches and damage. Never force anything, there is usually a reason if a part will not quite fit; for instance the lock plate will not set right in until the trigger has been pressed forward to clear the sear arm.

If a piece of wood has been broken off the fore part of a stock for instance, the best method of dealing with it is to cut out a clean shape and glue in a matching piece of wood that is a little larger than the final shape. When the piece of wood is securely glued it can be carved to shape with sharp chisels and gouges and finished with fine sandpaper. It may then need to be coloured and finished to match the remainder of the stock. Araldite is a very good glue for general repairs, being strong and waterproof, but as it takes some time to set, the work needs to be firmly held together until it is secure.

If a lathe is available this can be most useful for making ramrod tips, nipple keys, and various handles and knobs for tools and rods. If a lathe is not available there are now a number of firms specialising in antique gun parts who can supply a large variety of nipples, ramrod fittings, hammer blanks, gun furniture blanks, bullet moulds and many other useful pieces. They will of course copy a hammer or any other missing part but this sort of work can be costly.

Where a sword blade has much of its original finish and only a few rust spots the greatest care must be taken to preserve the original finish. The rust should first be worked off by careful scraping with something like the edge of a penny, and then the

Colour plate 24
Last stand of Kansuke.

remainder of the rust spots cleaned out. If the blade is of burnished or etched bright steel only, then it is comparatively simple to do the job with Duraglit which cleans and polishes without scratching. If, however, the blade is blued and gilt then, after surface rust spots have been worked off, careful work with a cleaning oil such as 3 in 1 will probably do the job best, because Duraglit would soon remove the blue and gilt finish.

Damascus or watered steel blades that have become rusted or have been buffed up bright can be restored by rubbing them down either with various grades of emery paper on a wooden block, or better with water stones of various degrees of fineness, until a good surface has been reached as free from rust pits as is practical. Obviously if there are some very deep pits there is a limit to the amount of metal that can be removed. On no account should this type of blade be buffed because the effect is to blur over the grain of the metal.

Assuming that the blade is now ready it must be completely degreased, ready for bringing out the pattern of the metal by the application of nitric acid. It is possible that originally only fruit acids were used to bring out the contrast in the metal of watered steel blades, but dilute nitric acid will achieve similar results. It is unlikely that a trough of acid will be available, therefore the acid may be applied with the aid of a cloth held in a protective glove and continuously wiped up and down the blade to keep the application even. Another method is to mix jewellers' rouge and acid together and paint this evenly on the blade, this prevents the tendency of the acid to run off some parts and come together in small globules in others. The rouge and acid treatment can be repeated, after washing the blade clean in cold water, until the right depth of contrast has been reached.

When the acid treatment is finished, wash the blade thoroughly in cold water and dry. When completely dry the blade should be wiped over with a light oil to seal the pores of the metal and when wiped clean the blade can be finished with a transparent wax. Blades should not be over oiled or smeared thickly with vaseline because this will be soaked up by leather or wooden scabbards and they will look messy and the beauty of the blade will be obscured.

There can be considerable difference between types of

166

watered steel found in Persian and Indian weapons; it can vary from a very fine grain with a slight contrast to a bold grain with a strong contrast between the bright globular cementite and the dark pearlite.

Where an iron hilt damascened or inlaid with gold or silver has become rusted, great care must be taken to avoid rubbing off the softer metal. The surface rust can be carefully worked off with a piece of copper and then the remainder cleaned out with Duraglit.

Kris blades may be found either rusted or rubbed smooth with emery cloth. Rust can be worked off with Duraglit without spoiling the etched effect, then when sufficiently clean it can be slightly oiled. If the blade had been rubbed smooth, then after cleaning and de-greasing, the best thing is to re-etch the blade with nitric acid until something of the original 'eaten away' appearance has been restored. Afterwards thoroughly wash, dry and lightly oil.

It is unfortunately only too common to find Japanese sword blades in a sorry state. Some have been chipped or badly scratched, others rubbed down with emery until their facets and all trace of the hardened edge, the grain and the burnished surfaces have been lost. Sometimes blades are found that have been buffed all over and even the russet tang polished up. The question of what to do for the best is a difficult one and must be decided on the merits of each individual blade. If it is a very good one then it will probably be best to send it to Japan for repolishing through a specialist dealer in this country.

If the blade has a few blemishes but sufficient original finish remains, then it may be best to leave it as it is.

Where a blade of a tanto or wakisashi has been rubbed down with emery or buffed, and it is not sufficiently valuable to send to Japan for re-polishing, then a collector may like to try his hand at the long and difficult task of restoring the blade to something like its original state.

First it is necessary to bring the blade up to a scratchless finish. This should be done by water stones, starting with coarse ones and working to very fine ones. A final finish may be aided by leather stuck to a piece of wood which has been damped and applied with jewellers' Diamantine. This could be followed by the use of jewellers' rouge.

At this stage the yakiba or hardened edge will usually show as a brighter area and the grain of the metal may show to a greater or lesser extent depending on the boldness of it. To bring out a fine grain it may be necessary to etch the blade very lightly and then polish this part with Duraglit and perhaps a little Diamantine. The yakiba that is bright at this stage can be restored to its frosted appearance by etching this part more deeply. This etch has to be painted on by mixing the acid with jewellers' rouge and painting it on most carefully with a water colour paint brush, following the hamon or outline of the yakiba. Nitric acid can be used for this purpose. The yakiba must only be worked on after etching with Duraglit because any hard polishing agent such as Diamantine would bring it up bright again obscuring the frosty granular structure caused by the water hardening and exposed by etching.

The parts of the blade normally burnished can be re-burnished with a hardened steel burnisher in strokes that go along the blade.

Quite reasonable results have been achieved by the writer on a number of blades but it is all very tricky work and as all blades do not respond in quite the same manner, a great deal of discretion and inovation may be necessary. Some blade collectors maintain that the Japanese polishers do not use etching as a means to bring out the yakiba but the writer has seen clear evidence, in swords returning from being re-polished in Japan, that at least some polishers etch the yakiba.

Even if the final results are not too good, a great deal will be learned about the blades in the course of trying to re-polish them that no amount of academic study will teach. As these blades have razor sharp edges, very great care must be taken in polishing if a nasty cut is to be avoided. One of the most difficult things to do, in restoring a blade of the normal type, is to re-shape the facets of the kissaki or angled tip of the blade. For this reason it is easier to start with a short blade that has flat sides.

The russet finish of a sword tang or a tsuba can be restored by controlled rusting, and shakudo or shibuichi that has been rubbed bright in places can be darkened to about the original blue black or silvery grey by dusting them over with sulphur and leaving them to patinate.

Restoration of weapons is a test of skill, ingenuity and

improvisation; it can certainly be very satisfying when well done. In the course of time much will be learned and quite a collection built up of tools and useful materials such as bits of iron and steel, brass, copper, silver, gold, gold leaf, leather, horn, antler, ivory, various woods, pearl shell and numerous other materials and things that can come in useful from time to time.

SOME TERMS EXPLAINED

CHASING Surface modelling of metal with chisels and punches.

DAMASCENING Encrusting metal, particularly iron with precious metals hammered onto a prepared (jagged up) surface.

DAMASCUS BARRELS, Eastern and European type—made by twisting together alternate rods of iron and steel which were then forged round a mandril. The name Damascus was given to them in error because of confusion with the origin of some sword blades of watered steel.

DAMASCUS STEEL or watered steel—swords and daggers forged from the famous wootz ingots from Hydrabad in India.

ENGRAVING Cutting lines into metal with a hardened steel graver.

INLAY Undercut channels or shapes which are filled with a softer precious metal.

LANGETS Small projections from the hilt over the top of the blade that fit either side of the scabbard top or locket.

QUILLON A sword guard composed of one or more bars between the hilt and blade.

REPOUSSÉ Method of working up a design from the back of sheet metal with punches and hammers; it is then finished from the front.

169

Books for further reference. (Currently in print).

General

1 Antique Weapons A-Z, Douglas J. Fryer, G. Bell & Sons.
2 Encyclopaedia of Firearms, H. L. Peterson, Connoisseur, London.
3 A History of Warfare, Field Marshal Viscount Montgomery of Alamein, Collins.
4 Swords and Daggers, F. Wilkinson, Ward Lock.

Chapter 1

British Pistols and Guns 1640–1840, Ian Glendenning, Arms and Armour Press.
Collecting Duelling Pistols, W. Keith Neal, Arms and Armour Press.
Forsyth & Co, Patent Gunmakers, W. Keith Neal and D. H. L. Back, G. Bell & Sons.
Rapiers, Eric Valentine, Arms and Armour Press.
Revolving Arms, A. W. F. Taylerson, Herbert Jenkins.
Small Swords and Military Swords, A. V. B. Norman, Arms and Armour Press.

Chapter 2

British Military Firearms 1650–1850, H. W. Blackmore, Herbert Jenkins.
The British Soldiers' Firearm 1850–1864, C. H. Roads, Herbert Jenkins.
British Military Swords, R. J. W. Latham, Hutchinson.
Militaria, F. Wilkinson, Ward Lock
Sword, Lance and Bayonet, C. Ffoulkes, Arms and Armour Press.

Chapter 3

Game Guns and Rifles, Percussion to Hammerless Ejector in Britain, R. Akehurst, G. Bell & Sons.
The Mantons, W. Keith Neal and D. H. L. Back, Herbert Jenkins.
Royal Sporting Guns at Windsor. H. L. Blackmore, H. M. Stationery Office.
Sporting Guns, R. Akehurst, Weidenfeld and Nicolson.

Chapter 4

Colt Firearms, 1836–1960, J. E. Serven, Santa Ana Cal. 1954.
Winchester, The Gun that Won the West, H. F. Williamson, Washington DC 1952.

Chapters 5 and 6

A Glossary of the Construction, Decoration and Use of Arms and Armour in all countries and in all times, together with some closely related subjects George Cameron Stone. Reprint by Jack Brussel New York.
Indian and Oriental Armour, Lord Egerton, Arms and Armour Press.

Chapter 7

The Arts of the Japanese Sword, B. W. Robinson, Faber & Faber.
Japanese Armour, L. J. Anderson, Arms and Armour Press.

Index

A

Adams, Robert, 29, 68
Algerian guns, 131
Amakuni, 150
Andrea Ferrara blades, 43
Anson and Deeley hammerless
   gun, 91
Arab sword, 126

B

Baghnak, 143
Baker, Ezekiel, 61
Baker rifle, 59
Baker, Sir Samuel, 98
Balkan guns, 133
Bayonet, socket, 50
Beesley, Frederick, 91
Belt pistols, Scottish, 43
Bichwa, 143
Big game rifles, 101
Bishop, William, 85
Bissell, Isaac, 56
Blunderbuss, 33, 133
Boar spear, 77
Bowie knife, 108
Boxer, Colonel, 68
Broadsword and Backsword,
   basket hilted, 8, 43

Brown Bess, 53
Brunswick rifle, 61
Buffalo Bill, 111
Bull-head mace, 133

C

Cadell, 46
Calisher and Terry, 67
Carbines, 55
Capping breech-loaders, 67
Cased pistols, 19
Cased sporting guns, 87
Cased sporting rifles, 98
Cavalry swords and sabres, 69
Centre-fire cartridge, 91
Ceylon, weapons from, 146
Chakram, 143
Christie, 46
Collier, Elisha, 24, 106
Colt revolvers, 106, 107
Colt, Samuel, 28, 68, 106
Conversion to percussion, 22
Copper cap, 21
Cossack and Georgian dagger,
   121
Cossack pistols, 133
Cromwell, Oliver, 48
Crow-bill axe, 140
Crutch sword, 140

INDEX

D

Damascus barrels, 93
Damascus or watered steel, 126
Daw, George, 91
Deer rifle, 97
Deringer, Henry, 118
Dirk, Scottish, 43
Double barrelled pistols, 24
Duck guns, 90
Duels, 19
Duelling pistols, 15

E

Egg, Durs, 16, 24
Egg, Joseph, 24
Enfield rifle, 64
English Civil War, 47
English dog-lock, 11

F

Ferguson's breech-loading rifle, 59
Ferguson, Captain, 59
Flintlock sporting guns, 79
Forsyth, Reverend, 21, 85
Four barrelled pistol, 31
Fowling pieces, 80
French flintlock, 12

G

Gibbs, George, 98

Griffin and Tow, 83
Guns, Scottish, 46

H

Hawker, Colonel, 84
Henry, Benjamin, 108
Highland Regiments, 56
Highland weapons, 38
Holster pistols, 12, 55
Howdah pistols, 31
Hunt, Walter, 108
Hunting sword, 77

I

Indian guns, 145
Indonesia, weapons from, 146
Infantry officers' swords, 70
Ironsides, 48

J

Jade hilts, 143
Jäger rifle, 96
Jambiya, 123
Japanese bow, 150
Japanese guns and pistols, 162
Japanese pole arms, 162
Japanese sword fittings, 158
Jezail, 145

K

Katana, 158

INDEX

Katar, 138
Kentucky rifle, 105
Ketland, 37
Khanda, 137
Kilij, 125
Korah, 140
Koto blades, 153
Kris, 147
Kukri knife, 140
Kyber knife, 138

L

Lancaster, Charles, 31, 87, 91, 112
Lang, Joseph, 19, 91
Lefaucheux breech-loader, 91
Left hand dagger, 8
Lloyd's patriotic fund swords, 75
Lochaber axe, 43
Lovell, George, 61

M

Mahomet's ladder, 130
Manton, John, 16, 24, 83
Manton, Joseph, 16, 83, 87
Marlborough, Duke of, 50
Martini-Henry rifle, 68
Masamune, 150
Masahide, 153
Matchlock sporting guns, 79
Merwin Hulbert & Co., 108
Minié rifled musket, 64
Miquelet lock, 131

Mortimer, 16
Mughal weapons, 143
Murdoch, John, 46
Musket, 'Brown Bess', 53
Musket, Duke of Richmond's pattern, 58
Musket, India pattern, 53

N

Naginatas, 162
Napoleonic Wars, 52
Naval officers' swords, 72
Naval weapons, 72
Needham, William, 91
Nelson, Admiral Horatio, 70
New Model Army, 48
Nock, Henry, 37, 56, 72, 83

O

Oakley, Annie, 112

P

Pata, 137
Peninsular Campaign, 52
Pepperbox, 25
Percussion ignition, 21
Pigeon guns, 90
Pinfire, 91
Pocket pistols, 15
Powder horns, Scottish, 46
Purdey, James, 33, 87, 91

INDEX

R

Rapier, 7
Remington, 108
Revolver, cased, 31
Revolver, flintl ·ck, 25
Revolver, percussion, 29, 68
Revolver, transitional, 27
Richards, Westley, 29, 67, 85
Rifle Regiment or 95th, 61
Rupert, Prince, 48

S

Sabre, 69
Samurai sword, 150
Seki style sword, 153
Set trigger, 16
Shamshir, 126
Shinkai, 153
Shinto blades, 153
Shooting galleries, 19
Skean dhu, 43
Small sword, 8
Smith and Wesson, 108
Snider, Jacob, 68
Spanish barrels, 80
Spencer repeating rifle, 108
Sporting guns and rifles, 79
Sukehiro, 153
Sukenao, 153
Sword of the armed knight of
    the Crusades, 7

T

Tachi, 150

Tanto, 150

Tanto, 150
Target pistols, 31
Tartar bow, 123
Tranter, 29
Trousse de chasse, 79
Tsuba, 158
Tulwar, 137
Turkish guns, 132
Turn-off pistols, 12
Twigg, John, 16, 83

V

Viking sword, 5
Volitional Repeater, 108

W

Wakizashi, 158
Waldpraxe, 79
Walker, Captain, 107
Webley, James, 29, 69
Wellington, Duke of, 52
Western legend, 111
Wheel-lock pistol, 11
Wheel-lock sporting guns, 79
Whitney, Eli, 107
Whitworth, Sir Joseph, 67
Whitworth rifle, 67
Winchester repeating rifle,
    108
Wogdon, Robert, 15
Wootz steel, 128

Y

Yataghan, 126

NOTES

NOTES

NOTES

NOTES